IOIB6336

"There Is An App For That!" provides spiritual applications for life challenges. Sufficiently explore biblical principles that SHIFT you into towering over every life challenge. Discern your spiritual season, what God requires of you in a given season, the purpose for the season and for life challenges, and how to successfully reap and triumph in every season of your life. You will also learn how to journey in your authority, seek respite in God, build a relationship with the Holy Spirit, while successfully fulfilling destiny assignments. There Is Indeed An App For That! And That! And That! And That!

THERE IS AN APP FOR THAT!
Spiritual Applications For Life Challenges

TaquettaBaker@Kingdomshifters.com

(Website) Kingdomshifters.com

Taquetta's Bio

Taquetta Baker is the founder of Kingdom Shifters Ministries (KSM). She has authored fourteen books and two decree CD's. Taquetta has a Master's Degree in Community Counseling with an emphasis on Marriage, Children and Family Counseling, a Bachelor's Degree in Psychology and Associates Degree in Business Administration. In addition, Taquetta has a Therapon Belief Therapist Certification from Therapon Institute and has 22 years of professional and Christian Counseling experience.

Taquetta is also gifted at empowering and assisting people with launching ministries, businesses and books and provides mentoring, counseling and vision casting through Kingdom Shifters Kingdom Wellness Program. Taquetta serves on the Board of Directors for New Day Community Ministries, Inc. of Muncie, IN. In October 2008, Taquetta graduated from the Eagles Dance Institute under Dr. Pamela Hardy and received her license in the area of liturgical dance. Before launching into her own ministry, Taquetta served at her previous church for 12 years. She was a prophet, pioneer and leader of Shekinah Expressions Dance Ministry, teacher, member of the presbytery board, and overseer of the Altar Workers Ministry. Taquetta receives mentoring and ministry covering from Bishop Jackie Green, Founder of JGM-National PrayerLife Institute (Phoenix, AZ), and was ordained as an Apostle on June 7, 2014.

Taquetta flows through the wells of warfare and worship and mantles an apostolic mandate of judging and establishing God's kingdom in people, ministries, communities, and regions. Taquetta travels in foreign missions and throughout the United States. She has mentored and established dance, altar workers, deliverance, and prophetic ministries. Taquetta ministers in the areas of fine arts, all manners of prayer, fivefold ministry, deliverance, healing, miracles, atmospheric worship, and empowers and train people in their destiny and life's vision.

Connect with Taquetta and KSM at kingdomshifters.com or via Facebook. For more information regarding Bishop Jackie Green at Jgmenternational.org.

Table of Contents

FORWARD

App software is a new term for those who are becoming more computer literate like myself. It means that whatever you want to create or support with an idea or vision; or manage better what you have, there is someone who has already created an "app software program" for that very purpose. Application software (apps) forms the backbone of many businesses. Some apps are free and some have to be purchased. I love the way author Taquetta Baker, makes it clear that there are some "Spiritual Apps" in the Word of God for whatever you are going through as a Christian. These spiritual apps are "free" because Jesus Christ has paid for them through His Blood. These are highly developed "holy apps" used by many Christians who have gone before us. She has packaged these apps for the reader in an excellent way.

THERE IS AN APP FOR THAT…is a powerful book and tool to reach generation now and generation next, who are searching and seeking for success. This book is FULL OF "WISDOM APPS" pointing the way to true discipleship in Jesus Christ. For the sinner who wants success without Christ, this book could transform their lives, and be the evangelist tool to receiving the "JESUS APP" to salvation.

I am honored to write the foreword for Taquetta's book for she has exemplified such wisdom coming from one so young. As one of my spiritual daughters, of whom I am most blessed to have, she has displayed wisdom beyond her years in the pages of this book. She is a prolific, prophetic and a profound biblical scholar in the Greek and Hebrew understanding of words and phrases to help the reader grow spiritually.

In the chapter "Seasons of Character Building," I loved the section on the 58 character traits of God. This "God App" on His character is truly the ones we can all share because we are made in His image. The author does spend time sharing on the traits that only God alone possesses. This chapter alone, however, could be a book, as with all her chapters.

In the closing chapter of her book, "The Holy Spirit As Friend," I was moved by the realization that these spiritual apps all require RELATIONSHIP WITH THE HOLY SPIRIT. Not just a moment in His Presence, but a lifestyle in His Presence. The author so eloquently states:
"God said that we tend to embrace the presence of the Holy Spirit, but have not received Him as our friend. This is huge within the body of Christ at present as praise and worship tends to be the center focus of Christendom. People are being touched Sunday after Sunday by the presence of God. However, the experiences are making us feel good in our flesh and emotions, but we leave out of services unchanged because we lack a true Spirit to Spirit encounter. This is because we are just encountering the presence of the Holy Spirit, but lack true relationship with the Him."

Every book that is written has a life to it and a purpose. This book is rich in scripture revelation and it is an "Everyday App Friendly" book for those who are babes in Christ, for those that are backslidden, for those that need refreshing and for those that need discipline in Christ. This book will never grow old or lose its power, for it is full of the Word, full of Wisdom and full of the Witness of the Holy Spirit upon it from page to page.

Endtime Vanguard Scribe,
Bishop Dr. Jackie L. Green
Founder/Overseer
JGM-Enternational PrayerLife Institute
Redlands, California and Phoenix, AZ

FORWARD

"There's An App For That" offers the promises and presence of God through a platform that we all understand – smart phone applications. Taquetta's latest book takes us into a contemporary world with declarations from ancient writings. Her writing powerfully challenges our thinking and compels us to become kingdom shifters. Through fasting and prayer, Taquetta picked up the heart of God's people and carried the burden to the throne of grace. This book is our reward from her intercession. She is a woman on a mission to see the body of Christ propelled into the supernatural. This book attacks mediocrity with a zero tolerance standard. Every word, every line, and every phrase is a power punch that delivers knockout blows to the demonic. On page after page, Taquetta inoculates us with phrases like glory light and soaking and shifting. This goes beyond simply putting on the armor of God; it arms us like soldiers prepared for war. This book walks each of us to the status of being more than a conqueror. The price of Taquetta's calling has been and continues to be extraordinarily high. There is no piece of advice or strategy that she presents in this book that did not first cost a season in the fire. To follow the tactics outlined in this book will escalate the reader's spiritual growth to light speed. This book is not for casual reading. It is for believers who want to know how to command the breaking of generational curses and speak in the authority of Jesus' name and live under a blood covering. The declarations in this book oblige the reader to become part of a worldwide revival movement. Taquetta has

mastered the scripture from Psalm 18:29 that she runs through troops and leaps over walls. It is impossible to talk with Taquetta for more than a few minutes and not hear her talk about miracles, signs, and wonders. She has the heart of a revolutionary warrior. With the spirit of a true leader, Taquetta has no contentment in resting in her own achievements but has a roaring hunger to impart to others what God has ordained in her. To describe Taquetta as an apostle, prophet, teacher, evangelist, pastor, healer, revivalist, psalmist, worshipper, intercessor, author, or commanding general of troops is accurate but still short of all that God has invested into her kingdom identity. Adding to her biological family, God has enriched her kingdom family with those who know her as mentor, sister, pastor, spiritual mother, colleague, or friend. I have been given the most incredible gift and privilege to have heaven allow me to know her as daughter.

Lovingly from Taquetta's Spiritual Mother,
Apostle Kathy E. Williams,
Founder of New Day Ministries, Muncie Indiana

FORWARD

"There's An App For That" is a book of very detailed, intricate, and intimate exploration. It is one that is birthed out of true experience. The knowledge, wisdom, and fruitfulness from this book has proven itself to be beyond effective and are truly needed. It is a weapon and ready tool for the body of Christ such that the bride can rise all the more and walk in greater victory over the infiltrations of darkness that has invaded not only the earth but our own personal and individual lives through life challenges. God's word tells us that to us it has been given to know the mysteries of the Kingdom of God (Luke 8:10). Mysteries in this scripture means hidden thing, secret, a hidden purpose or counsel, secret will, the secret counsels which govern God in dealing with the righteous. These mysteries, are hidden from the ungodly and wicked men but plain to the godly. Through the Holy Spirit and the voice of God that has prevailed through the author, this book does just that. It reveals many mysteries, counsels and encourages personal exploration, while also teaching how these mysteries apply and can be used in the daily lives of every person. It teaches on how God desires to govern his righteous people, while hiding all of his revealed mysteries from the discernment and hands of the enemy. Through this book God's word is made plain to us. It holds fresh revelation and truths to breaking through to walking in greater levels of victory, authority, godly character, healing, deliverance, and more as you walk the limitless and many times trying journey with God. Focuses such as being offensive against the enemy, discerning the seasons, knowing the reasons for life challenges, seasons of character building, and Holy Spirit are some of the topics that are explored in this book. It also emphasizes the importance of submitting yourself to the processes, seasons of learning and personal growth in which God may place you in so that Gods fruit can fully be made manifest in you through your challenges and in your life eternally. We declare an eternal work and establishing will take place as you journey in your exploration of this book. These teachings, prayers, decrees, and spiritual

explorations are ones that can be done multiple times to shift you into seeing the pure truth, and authority that exude from these applications, and we declare that they will become your first unction as trials and hardship arise in your life. In Jesus name, they will become your reality and bring about immediate transformation in you as the anointing and words from the pages breathe life, enlightenment, encouragement, and healing to you.

From Taquetta's Spiritual Daughter,
Nina Cook,
Founder of Manifold Grace Dance Company
Muncie, Indiana

THERE IS AN APP FOR THAT!

Spiritual Applications For Life Challenges

God has a remedy for every situation of life. He is the author and finisher of our lives and therefore, holds the key to assisting us with acquiring the victory we have already obtained from Jesus' work on the cross. Even as Jesus rose, we have risen with Him and have within us the power to successfully triumph in every life situation. In this book, we will explore biblical principles that **SHIFT** us into towering over every challenge in our lives. There Is Indeed An App For That! And That! And That! And That!

> *John 10:10*
> *The thief cometh not, but for to steal, and to kill, and to destroy: I am come that they might have life, and that they might have it more abundantly.*

> *Matthew 18:18*
> *Truly I tell you, whatever you bind on earth will be bound in heaven, and whatever you loose on earth will be loosed in heaven.*

Dictionary.com defines *Apply* as:

1. To make use of as relevant, suitable, or pertinent: to apply a theory to a problem.
2. To put to use, especially for a particular purpose
3. To bring into action; use; employ
4. To use a label or other designation
5. To use for or assign to a specific purpose: to put into effect

6. To devote or employ diligently or with close attention:

1Cor 4:15-16

For all things are for your sakes, that the abundant grace might through the thanksgiving of many redound to the glory of God. For which cause we faint not; but though our outward man perish, yet the inward man is renewed day by day.

Romans 8:28-30

And we know that all things work together for good to them that love God, to them who are the called according to his purpose. For whom he did foreknow, he also did predestinate to be conformed to the image of his Son, that he might be the firstborn among many brothers. Moreover whom he did predestinate, them he also called: and whom he called, them he also justified: and whom he justified, them he also glorified.

Hebrews 10:32-36 (The Message Version)

Remember those early days after you first saw the light? Those were the hard times! Kicked around in public, targets of every kind of abuse--some days it was you, other days your friends. If some friends went to prison, you stuck by them. If some enemies broke in and seized your goods, you let them go with a smile, knowing they couldn't touch your real treasure. Nothing they did bothered you, nothing set you back. So don't throw it all away now. You were sure of yourselves then. It's still a sure thing! But you need to stick it out, staying with God's plan so you'll be there for the promised completion.

Questions for Spiritual Exploration:

1. What current challenges are you facing?

2. What are the scriptures above speaking to you regarding your current situation?

3. What is God speaking to you personally as you are meditating on the scriptures above?

4. As you consider the definition, what does the word *"apply"* mean to you?

Offensive In Warfare

The word says *"Enter his gates with thanksgiving, enter his courts with praise"*
(Psalms 100:4). The word *enter* denotes an act of engagement. *Enter* means "to go into, infiltrate, intrude, creep in, make way, pierce, set foot in, pop in," **HELLO!** *Gates* represents a place or entry way into or within the heavenlies, and *courts* are a place of judgment and settlement. This means that even our adoration and praise unto God is an act of strategic engagement; acts of access and judgment! Our adoration and praise is our app...our password for annihilating the enemy!

> ### Psalms 100:4 (The Message Version)
> *Enter with the password: "Thank you!" Make yourselves at home, talking praise. Thank him. Worship him.*

Often we wait for the enemy to strike us, and then we seek to retaliate against what has been done against us. *Ephesians 6:12* states:

> *For we wrestle not against flesh and blood, but against principalities, against powers, against the rulers of the darkness of this world, against spiritual wickedness in heavenly places.*

Though Jesus has already brought us victory through His works on the cross, the enemy is continually seeking to take from us what is rightfully ours. He is also seeking to own whatever we have not claimed in our inheritance from the Lord. So though we have

4

won the war, we still wrestle the enemy who constantly contests us in making sure we do not walk in the full victory as heirs of God.

The reason our lives constantly feel like a war is because we tend to be defensive rather than offensive in claiming our kingly rights. We tend to wait until the enemy has something of ours then we have to fight Him to battle it back. We lack true pursuit in being offensive in claiming what is rightfully ours. Though the kingdom of heaven has suffered violence, Jesus has already taken the kingdom by force. Jesus blotted out the ordinances that were against us, that were contrary to us.

> *Colossians 2:13-15*
> *And you, being dead in your sins and the uncircumcision of your flesh, hath he quickened together with him, having forgiven you all trespasses; Blotting out the handwriting of ordinances that was against us, which was contrary to us, and took it out of the way, nailing it to his cross; And having spoiled principalities and powers, he made a shew of them openly, triumphing over them in it.*

> *The Message Version*
> *When you were stuck in your old sin-dead life, you were incapable of responding to God. God brought you alive — right along with Christ! Think of it! All sins forgiven, the slate wiped clean, that old arrest warrant canceled and nailed to Christ's cross. He stripped all the spiritual tyrants in the universe of their sham authority at the Cross and marched them naked through the streets.*

God is requiring us to be offensive as we enter His kingly gates...as we approach His heavenly courts. He is saying use your weapons (spiritual app) of thanks and praise to shift pass all that stands between you and me...all that prevents you from coming before me. God is saying, "I have already overpower it, overcame it, and so declare my justice by further shaming the enemy as you honor me."

When you thank God and praise Him, you are ascribing to the heavenlies that He is a good God, that He is God alone, and there is none comparable to Him. Your thanksgiving is attesting every devil that would try to get you to think otherwise of Him or to give into a lie that you are not victorious. Your praise is declaring that there is none like Him. There is none sovereign in rule but Him.

> **Isaiah 46:5 (The NET Version)**
> *To whom can you compare and liken me? Tell me whom you think I resemble, so we can be compared!*
>
> **The Message Version**
> *So to whom will you compare me, the Incomparable? Can you picture me without reducing me?*

WHEWWWWW! There is nothing in the universe we can reduce God to. Nothing can resemble or compare to Him! The minute you begin to assert your authority of praise, worship and thanksgiving while using this revelation, the battle is on yet the battle is won. The enemy will seek to prove you are wrong;

your God is not who you say He is; you do not really believe and live the life you declare. The enemy will attempt to assert heavenly jurisdiction over the area to which you are decreeing your blessings and judgment. The enemy will also strive to make sure you do not settle in a place he already feels is his or that he wants. Oh yes, he will attempt to battle with you and your incomparable God. Even as much, the enemy will endeavor to attack our relationship with God; however, in being offensive and strategically engaging in our app of praise, worship, and thanksgiving, we reduce the enemy to the footstool that he is....a defeated enemy.

Dictionary.com defines *Offensive* as:

1. Making attack, aggressive, relating to or designed for attack,
2. To be irritating or annoying, angering
3. Giving painful or unpleasant sensations : nauseous, obnoxious
4. Causing displeasure or resentment
5. The position or attitude of aggression or attack: an aggressive movement or attack:
6. Attempting to score or one up your opponent.
7. Disrespectful, insulting; displeasing
8. Synonyms: abusive, annoying, biting, cutting, detestable, disagreeable, discourteous, distasteful, dreadful, embarrassing, evil, foul, gross, hideous, horrible, horrid, impertinent, insolent, irritating, nauseating, objectionable, obnoxious, off-color, offending, outrageous, repellent, reprehensible,

repugnant, repulsive, revolting, rotten, rude, shocking, stinking, terrible, uncivil, unmannerly

❖ **On the defensive, you are trying to stop an opponent from their attack.**
❖ **On the offensive, you are striving to attack your opponent while gaining leverage or victory before being attacked.** So even now we SHIFT to a place of the victory, and must know that anything that opposes us is now illegal. The only hold it has on us is the hold we give to it in our in unrepented sin, or in our lack of not asserting our God-given authority over it.

Matthew 16:19
And I will give unto thee the keys of the kingdom of heaven: and whatsoever thou shalt bind on earth shall be bound in heaven: and whatsoever thou shalt loose on earth shall be loosed in heaven.

Romans 6:9
For we know that since Christ was raised from the dead, he cannot die again; death no longer has mastery over him.

Ways of Being Offensive

- Enter God's presence with praise and thanksgiving, while utilizing your authority to release judgment of who God is and what He has done and will do in your life.
- Make a list of who He is and what the word says about Him and declare it out loud as this

ascribes to the heavenlies who He is….the incomparable God.

- Spend consistent time soaking and being transparent in the presence of God. As you soak, absorb who He is; declare that you are becoming who you say He is. You are becoming His might, His strength, His matchless power. An example of this type of prayer is as followed:
    - o I soak in You Lord. I declare You are all mighty and I absorb Your might right now. I decree I am being drenched and overtaken in Your sensational power and might. And even as Your word says I am made in Your image, I decree I am mounting up in Your might right now in Jesus name. Demons and all that is not of You is loosing me, because I am surrendering and being captivated by Your might that contends and speaks for me. More consumption Jesus, more saturation Jesus, more immersing in Your might Father. I rest in Your might and just relax in you as Your might overtakes and empowers me.
- Consistently repent and acknowledge your own sin and let God cleanse, deliver and heal you. You do this by searching out your own generational curses and strongholds, and seeking God for deliverance of them, rather than waiting until the enemy exposes or binds you.
- Be proactive and pray strategic prayers that send the devil's mess back to him.

Questions for Spiritual Exploration:

1. What position of authority did Jesus' work on the cross gain for your life?"

2. What do you need to do to practice living from this authoritative place Jesus shifted you into?

3. What revelation did you gain about Psalms 100:4 and the weapons (spiritual apps) of praise, worship, and thanksgiving?

4. As you consider your situation, how can you use these spiritual apps to assert authority over your present challenges?

Offensive Decree To Dispel The Enemy

1. Jesus, I boldly enter Your gates with thanksgiving and enter Your courts with praise. I declare You are Lord. You are Savior, You are King! I declare that You have done great works and that there is none like You in the entire universe. I declare You are for me. You are with me. You are my God and all others are reduced counterfeits, groping at Your feet.

2. I decree the universe is Yours and all belongs to You. I thank You for making the world and for giving me jurisdiction to subdue, multiply and have dominion. I thank You for giving me authority to establish Your kingdom in the earth (Genesis 1:28).

3. I thank You that even as the devil wanders, He is subject to Your authority and power in me. Thank You Jesus for giving me power over all the power of the darkness and every demonic entity (Luke 10:19).

4. Even as I have thanked You and ascribed unto You worthy praise, I offensively take my stance as an ambassador of Your kingdom.

5. I decree even now that my adversaries are being clothed with shame. They are being eternally covered with confusion even now. The mantle of confusion and shame is overtaking them even now (Psalms 109:29).

6. I decree Lord that my accusers are being totally disgraced and wrapped in shame as with a cloak.

7. May all who gloat over my distress be put to shame and confusion; may all who exalt themselves over me be clothed with shame and disgrace (Psalm 35:26).

8. Lord I decree that the devils who curse me, wear their own cursing as a garment. I decree their own curses boomerang back unto them, while infiltrating their own camp with sevenfold discourse, girdling and annihilation (Psalm 109:17-20).

9. Be pleased, O Lord, to deliver (defend, rescue) me: O Lord, make haste to help me. Let them be ashamed and confounded (embarrassed, reproached) together that seek after my soul to destroy it; let them be driven backward and put to shame that wish me evil. Let them be desolate for a reward of their shame and confusion that say unto me, Aha, aha (Psalms 35:4-12Psa 40:13-15, Psalm 63:9, Psalm 71:13).

10. Even as the word *desolate* is "*Samem*" in the Hebrew and means to be desolate, appalled, stun, stupefy, horror, horror-causer, deflowered, ravaged, astounded, ruined; I decree Your presence enters my sphere to stun and stupefy the enemy. I decree Your presence arise in a horror and exert how appalled You are at the enemy's tactics against me and all that concerns me. I decree that Your presence ravage and ruin the plots and plans of the enemy against me and my sphere, while releasing Your justice on my behalf.

11. For though the wicked are waiting to destroy me, I trust You to avenge me as I exalt You and ponder Your statutes. I posture in offense and surrender my opponents to You. They do not move me in their treacherous endeavors, for I am only concerned with Your plans for me. I see the limits to everything human and demonic, but the horizons can't contain Your commands or Your ways. You are without limits and Your plans are never obsolete (Psalm 119:95-106, The Message Version).

12. For my enemies are unfulfilled, dismayed and despaired. It is because You are the incomparable God and the stance of my life. I ground myself in thanks and praise unto You. I bellow Your awesomeness in defense against the enemy (Jeremiah 14:3).

13. Thank You Lord for being the annihilator, the abolisher, the extinguisher of all things evil (Psalms 68:21).

14. Thank You for exterminating the enemy and liquidating his filthy in my life and sphere.

15. You are my God and it is You that I will continually exalt and praise (Hebrew 13:15, Psalms 34:1).

Discerning The Seasons

Ecclesiastes 3:1-5

For everything there is a season, and a time for every matter under heaven: a time to be born, and a time to die; a time to plant, and a time to pluck up what is planted; a time to kill, and a time to heal; a time to break down, and a time to build up; a time to weep, and a time to laugh; a time to mourn, and a time to dance; a time to cast away stones, and a time to gather stones together; a time to embrace, and a time to refrain from embracing;

Daniel 2:21

He changes times and seasons; he removes kings and sets up kings; he gives wisdom to the wise and knowledge to those who have understanding;

Genesis 8:22

While the earth remains, seedtime and harvest, cold and heat, summer and winter, day and night, shall not cease."

Acts 1:7

He said to them, "It is not for you to know times or seasons that the Father has fixed by his own authority.

Matthew 24:32

"From the fig tree learn its lesson: as soon as its branch becomes tender and puts out its leaves, you know that summer is near.

Jeremiah 5:24-25
They do not say in their hearts, 'Let us fear the Lord our God, who gives the rain in its season, the autumn rain and the spring rain, and keeps for us the weeks appointed for the harvest.' Your iniquities have turned these away, and your sins have kept good from you.

The Message Version
It never occurs to them to say, 'How can we honor our God with our lives, The God who gives rain in both spring and autumn and maintains the rhythm of the seasons, Who sets aside time each year for harvest and keeps everything running smoothly for us?'

Every aspect of our lives, whether personal, relationships, marriages, churches, ministries, jobs, etc., are impacted by seasons and transitions.

Seasons affect everything about us. Seasons determine:
- What we accomplish as some seasons we are able to get more done than others.
- What we wear as depending on the season, we wear more clothing and our style and attire changes depending on the season.
- Our mood as if we enjoy a season, we are more joyful, encouraged and empowered. We may have to press through in our mood and character with seasons we are not fond of.
- Our interactions as depending on what is occurring we may be less or more available to others.

Everything about us is impacted by spiritual and natural seasons. Spiritually, if you are able to discern your season, then you can more effectively maneuver through life challenges and changes.

Spiritual seasons are designed by God. They are not dictated by the natural seasons of winter, spring, summer and fall. Though naturally one could be in a particularly season such as summer, spiritually a person could be experiencing an entirely different season like spring or winter. In the natural we tend to prepare for upcoming seasons. We conduct spring cleaning, purchase winter and summer clothing, prepare for the school year, etc. Even as we consider such preparation, it is essential therefore, to be fervent in also preparing for spiritual seasons. It is important to seek God for revelation of one's spiritual season. It is moreover, important to discern the patterns of your spiritual seasons so you can prepare beforehand for seasons you are in or entering into. This will assist with conquering or weathering challenges that occur as seasons unfold.

Naturally, some seasons reap more harvest than others. For instance, farmers tend to reap more in the spring and summer than in the winter and fall. However, spiritually, it is possible to yield fruit in every spiritual season. This however, requires recognizing what season you are in and how to sufficiently sow into that season to reap fruit.

Psalm 1:3
He is like a tree planted by streams of water that
yields its fruit in its season, and its leaf does not
wither. In all that he does, he prospers.

Jeremiah 17:8
They will be like a tree planted by the water that
sends out its roots by the stream. It does not fear
when heat comes; its leaves are always green. It has
no worries in a year of drought and never fails to
bear fruit."

Ezekiel 19:10
Your mother was like a vine in your vineyard
planted by the water; it was fruitful and full of
branches because of abundant water.

Ezekiel 31:5
So it towered higher than all the trees of the field; its
boughs increased and its branches grew long,
spreading because of abundant waters.

Ezekiel 47:12
Fruit trees of all kinds will grow on both banks of
the river. Their leaves will not wither, nor will their
fruit fail. Every month they will bear fruit, because
the water from the sanctuary flows to them. Their
fruit will serve for food and their leaves for healing.

As you can see from the scriptures, this also requires
tapping into the waters of God. As just like natural
seasons, it rains in every season. Our natural and
spiritual seasons/lives cannot live without water.
Water is essential to sustain life and is necessary for
producing quality harvest.

Isaiah 58:11
The LORD will guide you always; he will satisfy your needs in a sunscorched land and will strengthen your frame. You will be like a wellwatered garden, like a spring whose waters never fail.

Ezekiel 47:9
Swarms of living creatures will live wherever the river flows. There will be large numbers of fish, because this water flows there and makes the salt water fresh; so where the river flows everything will live.

John 7:37-38
In the last day, that great day of the feast, Jesus stood and cried, saying, If any man thirst, let him come to me, and drink. 38He that believes on me, as the scripture has said, out of his belly shall flow rivers of living water.

John 4:14
But whoever drinks the water I give them will never thirst. Indeed, the water I give them will become in them a spring of water welling up to eternal life.

Expect and pursue harvest in each season. God is a continually blessing God and He does not stop blessing. Even in the wilderness, the Israelites received great outpourings of God's glory, manna from heaven, and miracle after miracle. The Word says that for forty years, their clothing never wore out. In spiritual lingo, we consider the wilderness to be a dry, lonely season that lacks harvests. Yet even in the midst of learning to lean on God, the Israelites, experienced great spiritual and natural harvest and provision. It is essential that we grasp that as we follow God, there is no lack. He is a constant provider and source. He is all about edifying us, accelerating us, and transforming us into what He created us to be.

> *Deuteronomy 8:1-5*
> *All the commandments which I command thee this day shall ye observe to do, that ye may live, and multiply, and go in and possess the land which the LORD sware unto your fathers. And thou shalt remember all the way which the LORD thy God led thee these forty years in the wilderness, to humble thee, and to prove thee, to know what was in thine heart, whether thou wouldest keep his commandments, or no. And he humbled thee, and suffered thee to hunger, and fed thee with manna, which thou knewest not, neither did thy fathers know; that he might make thee know that man doth not live by bread only, but by every word that proceedeth out of the mouth of the LORD doth man live. Thy raiment waxed not old upon thee, neither did thy foot swell, these forty years.*

Questions for Spiritual Exploration:

1. What is the difference between spiritual and natural seasons?
2. What does the bible say about reaping in every season?
3. What spiritual season you are in and what are the characteristics of this season?
4. What are some patterns you see as you consider the spiritual seasons your life encounter?

Knowing God's Seasonal Requirements

What is God requiring of you in the season you are in? This is an important question in obtaining the lesson, fruit, and provision needed to sustain and accelerate efficiently and proficiently. Let us explore some apps that will enable us to discern what God is requiring so we can discern and obtain the fruit of our season.

Faith Walk:

At times when we are in a season of faith, God may not speak. He may be sharpening our spiritual knowing. A spiritual knowing is a confidence in our spirit in which we know that God is with us and will do what He says, even though He is not speaking. Is God sharping your spiritual knowing? Is God teaching you how to walk by faith? Is He teaching you how to lean and trust in Him and to please Him? Is He teaching you how to lean on His promises and take comfort in Him as Your God?

☐ *Galatians 2: 16* Knowing that a man is not justified by the works of the law but by faith in Jesus Christ, even we have believed in Christ Jesus, that we might be justified by faith in Christ and not by the works of the law; for by the works of the law no flesh shall be justified.

☐ *Hebrews 11: 6* - But without faith it is impossible to please Him, for he who comes to God must believe that He is, and that He is a rewarder of those who diligently seek Him.

- *Psalm 119:50* - My comfort in my suffering is this: Your promise preserves my life.
- *1Corinthians 2: 5* - So that your faith might not rest in the wisdom of men (human philosophy), but in the power of God.
- *James 1: 3* - Be assured and understand that the trial and proving of your faith bring out endurance and steadfastness and patience.
- *2 Corinthians 5: 7* - For we walk by faith, not by sight.

Fulfilling Prophecy & Following the Voice of God:
Is this a season of walking in what God has already spoken? Is this a season of walking out the voice and prophecies of God? Is this a season of knowing and standing on the word of God?

Psalm 119:114-115 You are my refuge and my shield; I have put my hope in your word. Away from me, you evildoers, that I may keep the commands of my God!

☐ *Psalm 119:25* I am laid low in the dust; preserve my life according to your word.

☐ *Jeremiah 29:11* - For I know the plans I have for you," declares the Lord, "plans to prosper you and not to harm you, plans to give you hope and a future.

☐ *Isaiah 55:10-11* - For as the rain and the snow come down from heaven and do not return there but water the earth, making it bring forth and sprout, giving seed to the sower and bread to the eater, so shall my word be that goes out from my mouth; it shall not return to me empty, but it shall accomplish that which I purpose, and shall succeed in the thing for which I sent it.

☐ *Psalm 119:71* - It was good for me to be afflicted so that I might learn your decrees.

Taking a Kingdom Stance:
Often we do not like to just stand in the truth of God. It tends to be a season of receiving contention from the enemy and people, yet we are simply required to stand in the truth of what He has spoken or said in His word and let our stance speak for itself. We do not deem this productive yet, in the natural if you stand on your legs long enough, you are able to stretch and assert jurisdiction in the place to which

you are standing. This is the same in the spirit and even more so, because you are physically a representation, a banner, a contender for God's kingdom.

- ☐ *Psalm 16:8* - I have set the LORD always before me. Because he is at my right hand, I will not be shaken.
- ☐ *Luke 21:19* – By standing firm you will win
- ☐ your souls.

  Ephesians 6:10-17 - Finally, my brethren, be strong in the Lord and in the power of His might. Put on the whole armor of God that you may be able to stand against the wiles of the devil. For we do not wrestle against flesh and blood, but against principalities, against powers, against the rulers of the darkness of this age, against spiritual hosts of wickedness in the heavenly places. Therefore take up the whole armor of God that you may be able to withstand in the evil day, and having done all, to stand. Stand therefore, having girded your waist with truth, having put on the breastplate of righteousness, and having shod your feet with the preparation of the gospel of peace; above all, taking the shield of faith with which you will be able to quench all the fiery darts of the wicked one. And take the helmet of salvation, and the sword of the Spirit, which is the word of God;

Godly Maturation:

Sometimes, it may feel as if God is causing us to consume a lot of information at one time. It may feel as if we are consuming so much knowledge, until we do not have time to process it all, and may not even understand all God is doing. However, when we are in this season, God is maturing us for a greater work. There will be seasons of great consumption so that as we grow, we can be equipped with the tools to sustain in the future. We will also be able to adequately impart into others, what God has downloaded into us. This season at times require great sacrifice and accepting the responsibility that comes with the calling on our lives. When we are children, we tend to lean on others, but as we age, we incur more responsibility and independence. We play less, and have to be more responsible in how we use our time and in making sure we are learning and maturing in the necessary areas to successfully advance in life. Though there is continual joy in being in God's will, we are required to shift with God so we can be equipped to advance His kingdom. If God is drawing to constantly study, praying, fast, attend workshops, etc., explore whether you are in a season of maturity.

- ☐ *1 Corinthians 13:11* - When I was a child, I spoke like a child, I thought like a child, I reasoned like a child. When I became a man, I gave up childish ways.

- ☐ *Hebrews 5:12-14* - For though by this time you ought to be teachers, you need someone to teach you again the basic principles of the oracles of God. You need milk, not solid food, for everyone who lives on milk is unskilled in the word of righteousness, since he is a child. But solid food is for the mature, for those who have their powers of discernment trained by constant practice to distinguish good from evil.

☐ *Psalm 138:8* - The Lord will fulfill his purpose for me; your steadfast love, O Lord, endures forever. Do not forsake the work of your hands.
1Corinthians 14:20 - Brothers, do not be children in your thinking. Be infants in evil, but in your thinking be mature.

☐ *Ephesians 4:11-14* - And he gave the apostles, the prophets, the evangelists, the shepherds and teachers, to equip the saints for the work of ministry, for building up the body of Christ, until we all attain to the unity of the faith and of the knowledge of the Son of God, to mature manhood, to the measure of the stature of the fullness of Christ, so that we may no longer be children, tossed to and fro by the waves and carried about by every wind of doctrine, by human cunning, by craftiness in deceitful schemes.

☐ *John 15:2* - Every branch in me that does not bear fruit he takes away, and every branch that does bear fruit he prunes, that it may bear more fruit.

☐ *Luke 2:52* - And Jesus increased in wisdom and in stature and in favor with God and man.

- *Proverbs 1:5* -Let the wise hear and increase in learning, and the one who understands obtain guidance.
- *Proverbs 18:15* - An intelligent heart acquires knowledge, and the ear of the wise seeks knowledge.
- *2 Timothy 3:16* - All Scripture is breathed out by God and profitable for teaching, for reproof, for correction, and for training in righteousness.
- *2 Timothy 2:15* - Do your best to present yourself to God as one approved, a worker who has no need to be ashamed, rightly handling the word of truth.

Decreeing & Declaring:

Though we should consistently stand on and decree out God's word and promises, there are seasons where this app is necessary to acquire the fruit and manifestation of God and His kingdom. We will be required to habitually decree out what God has spoken in intercession and warfare, and stand in the truth of what He has spoken despite our circumstances. Often we despise the constant prayer repetition that this particular season demands. It is important to know that the word and thoughts of God are actual devices, machines, and inventions. Physical matter is manifesting through them, while birthing forth the literal thoughts, plans and desires of God. *Psalms 92:5 O Lord, how great are thy works! And thy thoughts are very deep.*

Thoughts in the Hebrew is _Machashebeth_ and means:

1. A contrivance which means to plan with ingenuity; devise; invent
2. A texture, machine, or intention,
3. Plan (whether bad, a plot; or good, advice): — cunning (work), curious work,
4. Device (- sed), imagination, invented,
5. A means, purpose, work, imaginations, invention

God's words carry His texture which is His spirit and His image. That is the reason He says they will not return void. As God's words are spoken, His spirit and image, begins to form and materialize the purpose to which they were sent, and anything that is resisting them is counterattacked by His breath (Spirit) being on them.

When God created the world, He spoke it forth. As He spoke, His word snuffed out any void and darkness, while forming His light and His desires. This is what decreeing and speaking God's word does for us. Yet unlike God, we are not perfect. We may have to contend in prayer and keep decreeing in order to snuff out the darkness in us and around us, such that His light and will births forth in our midst. Also, the devil roams seeking whom he can devour, so he will attempt to resist what God has for us (study Daniel 10). The devil knew better than to resist God when the world was being formed, as the devil had already been put out of heaven. Satan eagerly approached Eve and actually used a play on words to get her to eat from the tree of good and evil. Unlike God, the devil's words only have power if we give power to them.

Seasons of decreeing can birth an abundance of fruit and breakthrough that can manifest in future seasons. It is you making a conscious decision to agree with God so He can establish His plans in your midst. If things are not manifesting, keep decreeing them until you have confirmation and/or a release in your spirit that they have been spiritually birthed, and will come to pass in your natural life.

> *Job 22:26-28* - You shall make your prayer to him, and he shall hear you, and you shall pay your vows. You shall also decree a thing, and it shall be established to you: and the light shall shine on your ways. Whatever you decide on a matter, it will be established for you, and light will shine on your ways. (NET)

- *Ephesians 6:18* -Praying at all times in the Spirit, with all prayer and supplication. To that end keep alert with all perseverance, making supplication for all the saints.
- *Ezekiel 26:9* - And he shall set battering rams against your walls, and with his axes he shall break down your towers.
  - *New Living Translation* - He will direct the blows of his battering rams against your walls and demolish your towers with his weapons.

The Kingdom Press:

There are times when we are in a season of pressing to another level and dimension in God. We are not quite where we should be, and it takes a deep pressing to get to where God is taking us. This season can be challenging, but our fruit resides in the press.

Press in the Greek is *Dio* and means:

1. To flee; to pursue (literally or figuratively); by implication, to persecute: — ensue, follow (after), given to, (suffer) persecute (- ion), press forward, suffer persecution

2. To make to run or flee, put to flight, drive away to run swiftly in order to catch a person or thing, to run after to press on

3. One who in a race runs swiftly to reach the goal to pursue (in a hostile manner) in any way whatever to harass, trouble, molest one

4. To persecute to be mistreated, suffer persecution on account of something

5. Without the idea of hostility, to run after, to pursue to seek after eagerly, earnestly endeavor to acquire

Pressing requires sweat, hard work and even tears. It is a constant pursue of a goal despite hardship and persecution. As we are pressing, we are maturing in our spiritual fruit, stamina and being able to remain constant and focused on the word. We are also accelerating upward, so there is another level of authority and power we are attaining. In addition as we press forward, the things behind us loose us and no longer become a factor as our stride and eyes are on what lies ahead. Are you in a kingdom press? What is the level are you attaining in God? As you thrust forward, what dimension of glory has He promised you?

☐ *Philippians 3:12-14* - Not as though I had already attained, either were already perfect: but I follow after, if that I may apprehend that for which also I am apprehended of Christ Jesus. Brothers, I count not myself to have apprehended: but this one thing I do, forgetting those things which are behind, and reaching forth to those things which are before, I press toward the mark for the prize of the high calling of God in Christ Jesus.

☐ *Luke 9:62* - Jesus replied, "No one who puts a hand to the plow and looks back is fit for service in the kingdom of God."

☐ *Hebrews 6:1* - Therefore let us move beyond the elementary teachings about Christ and be taken forward to maturity, not laying again the foundation of repentance from acts that lead to death, and of faith in God.

☐ *II Corinthians 2:18* - But we all, with unveiled face, beholding as in a mirror the glory of the Lord, are being transformed into the same image from glory to glory, just as from the Lord, the Spirit.

Divine Rest:

We will discuss divine rest in detail later in this book; however, let us consider whether you are in a season of rest? Is this a time of refreshing, restoration and absorbing the healing power of God?

Rest in the Greek is *Anapauo* and means to:

1. Reflexively) to repose (literally or figuratively (be exempt), remain)
2. To refresh: — take ease, refresh, (give, take) rest.
3. To cause or permit one to cease from any movement or labor in order To recover and collect his strength
4. To give rest, refresh, to give one's self rest, take rest
5. To keep quiet, of calm and patient expectation

Rest in the Greek is also *Anapausis* and means:

1.   Intermission; by implication, recreation, rest
2.   Cessation of any motion, business or labor rest, recreation

Many have a difficult time resting because they are so use to doing and going. Some are not use to being by themselves or spending time alone. Then there are others that do not like themselves and therefore, when it is quiet and they are with themselves, they do not know how to embrace the power that resides in resting. It is essential, however, to surrender to seasons of rest and even take days of refreshing when

31

you are feeling tired, overwhelmed, and anxious.
When we cease from our works, God is able to cleanse
and heal us from the warfare, hurts, anxiety, burnout,
sin and soulish issues, etc. He is also able to refresh
us and speak further direction and clarity for what
lies ahead. The strength of God's voice rests in the
stillness.

- ☐ *Matthew 11:28-29* - Come unto me, all ye that labor and are heavy laden, and I will give you rest. Take my yoke upon you, and learn of me; for I am meek and lowly in heart: and you will find rest unto your souls.
- ☐ *Exodus 33:14* - My presence will go with you,
- ☐ and I will give you rest.

  Psalm 62:1-2 - My soul finds rest in God alone; my salvation comes from him. He alone is my rock and my salvation; he is my fortress, I will never be shaken.
- ☐ *Isaiah 40:28- 31* - Do you not know? Have you not heard? The Lord is the everlasting God, the Creator of the ends of the earth. He will not grow tired or weary, and his understanding no one can fathom. He gives strength to the weary and increases the power of the weak. Even youths grow tired and weary, and young men stumble and fall; but those who hope in the Lord will renew their strength. They will soar on wings like eagles; they will run and not grow weary, they will walk and not be faint."
- ☐ *Hebrews 4: 9-11* - Let us therefore strive to enter that rest, so that no one may fall by the same sort of disobedience.

- *1 Peter 5:7* - Casting all your anxieties on him, because he cares for you.
- *Psalm 62:5* - Yes, my soul, find rest in God: my hope comes from him.
- *Psalm 116:7* - Return to your rest, my soul, for the Lord has been good to you.
- *Mark 6:31* - Then, because so many people were coming and going that they did not even have a chance to eat, he said to them, "Come with me by yourselves to a quiet place and get some rest.
- *1 John 3:19* - This is how we know that we belong to the truth and how we set our hearts at rest in his presence.
- *1 Peter 3:4* - Rather, it should be that of your inner self, the unfading beauty of a gentle and quiet spirit, which is of great worth in God's sight.
- *Psalm 131:2* - But I have calmed and quieted myself, I am like a weaned child with its mother; like a weaned child I am content.

Divine Concealing/Protection:

Sometimes, God will place us in a season where He conceals us.

- He may hide us in a church where no one understands or recognize our giftings. (You think you are just being overlooked but God is hiding you while He cultivates you for a greater work).
- He may hide us from people or the world so they cannot taint the work that He is doing in us. (You think you do not have

any friends because you are misunderstood or your mate is never coming because no one approaches you, but God has you hidden to keep you pure and to have time with you unto Himself)

o He may require us to move to a place where we have no family or friends. (You think it is because your family is just crazy and you have to get away from them, but God is strategically positioning you to take over a region).

o He may hide us from unforeseen warfare (*2Corinthians 1:10* *The Amplified Versions - [For it is He] Who rescued and saved us from such a perilous death, and He will still rescue and save us; in and on Him we have set our hope (our joyful and confident expectation) that He will again deliver us [from danger and destruction and draw us to Himself]*. This season tends to feel like we are in a wilderness or an isolated cave. And we may not recognize that it is for our own good, because we are focused on our temporary emotions, desires and feelings, rather than God's future plan. God is all about the future, the generations, and the eternal. Unless He states otherwise, He is constantly equipping us for what resides ahead. What we are doing through us today most likely a result of past seasons of imparting, empower, and building. His work tends to be on where we are going and making sure we are prepared for what lies ahead.

- *Proverbs 18:10* - The name of the LORD is a strong tower; the righteous run to it and are safe.
- *Ephesians 1:11* - In him we have obtained an inheritance, having been predestined according to the purpose of him who works all things according to the counsel of his will.
- *1 Samuel 2:9* - He will keep the feet of his saints, and the wicked shall be silent in darkness; for by strength shall no man prevail.
- *Psalm 18:30* - As for God, His way is perfect; the word of the Lord is proven; He is a shield to all who trust in Him.
- *Psalm 31:20* - You shall hide them in the secret place of Your presence from the plots of man; You shall keep them secretly in a pavilion from the strife of tongues.
- *Psalm 32:7* - You are my hiding place; You shall preserve me from trouble; You shall surround me with songs of deliverance.

Birthing:

Are you in a season of building a foundation or birthing forth a ministry, vision, gifting, character, a generation, etc.? What is it that you are birthing? What reasons are you in this birthing process? What are the characteristics or fruit God is planting in your foundation? What is it you need from God or to be done in you to successfully deliver and build a solid foundation for that which you are birthed?

- ☐ *Luke 23:29* - For behold, the days are coming when they will say, 'Blessed are the barren and the wombs that never bore and the breasts that never nursed!'
- ☐ *Genesis 3:16* - To the woman he said, "I will surely multiply your pain in childbearing; in pain you shall bring forth children. Your desire shall be for your husband, and he shall rule over you."
- ☐ *Genesis 1-28* - And God blessed them, and God said unto them, Be fruitful, and multiply, and replenish the earth, and subdue it: and have dominion over the fish of the sea, and over the fowl of the air, and over every living thing that moveth upon the earth.

Building & Investing (Plowing) (read Nehemiah 4):
Building requires diligence, teamwork, consistency, and continual construction and cultivation of the vision. Building also encompasses following the strategic plan and steps of the Lord, even operating in those directions that do not make sense in the natural.

- ☐ *Proverbs 9:1* - Wisdom has built her house; she has set up its seven pillars.
- ☐ *Proverbs 31:10-31* - An excellent wife who can find? She is far more precious than jewels. The heart of her husband trusts in her, and he will have no lack of gain. She does him good, and not harm, all the days of her life. She seeks wool and flax, and works with willing hands.

She is like the ships of the merchant; she brings her food from afar.

- **1Corinthians 3:9** - For we are God's fellow workers. You are God's field, God's building.
- **Matthew 15:13** - He replied, Every plant that my heavenly Father has not planted will be pulled up by the roots.
- **Psalms 65:8-10** – They who dwell in the ends of the earth stand in awe of Your signs; You make the dawn and the sunset shout for joy. You visit the earth and cause it to overflow; You greatly enrich it; The stream of God is full of water; You prepare their grain, for thus You prepare the earth. You water its furrows abundantly, You settle its ridges, You soften it with showers, You bless its growth.

Maturing a Ministry or Vision:

This is a season of stabilizing the foundation by equipping and growing self and others so that the ministry or vision can sustain throughout generations. It may require revamping the ministry or vision by stripping things that are not fruitful and providing new strategies that will help advance the ministry or vision.

- **Ephesians 4:11-13** - And He Himself gave some to be apostles, some prophets, some evangelists, and some pastors and teachers, for the equipping of the saints for the work of ministry, for the edifying of the body of Christ, till we all come to the unity of the faith and of the knowledge of the Son of God, to a perfect man, to the measure of the stature of the fullness of Christ;

- *2Timothy 4:5* - But watch thou in all things, endure afflictions, do the work of an evangelist, make full proof of thy ministry
  - But you watch in all things, endure afflictions, do the work of an evangelist, fully carry out your ministry (KJV)
- *Jeremiah 31:16* -This is what the LORD says: "Restrain your voice from weeping and your eyes from tears, for your work will be rewarded," declares the LORD. "They will return from the land of the enemy.
- *Ephesians 2: 21* - In Him the whole structure is joined (bound, welded) together harmoniously, and it continues to rise (grow, increase) into a holy temple in the Lord [a sanctuary dedicated, consecrated, and sacred to the presence of the Lord].
- *Mark 4:8* - And other seed [of the same kind] fell into good (welladapted) soil and brought forth grain, growing up and increasing, and yielded up to thirty times as much, and sixty times as much, and even a hundred times as much as had been sown.

Sowing:

There are seasons where we simply sow and give out in ministry. We give of our time, giftings, finances, etc., and our learning and reward is in what we give out, or even may come in future seasons. It is important to discern this season as often we will become frustrated because we may not receive personally in our study, or from our assembly, and there is a constant giving out with minimal personal watering. But God promises that our sowing is not in vain, and that if we give unto others, He will reap unexplainable rewards.

- *Proverbs 11:24-25* - One person gives freely, yet gains even more; another withholds unduly, but comes to poverty. A generous person will prosper; whoever refreshes others will be refreshed.
  - The liberal person shall be enriched, and he who waters shall himself be watered. The people curse him who holds back grain [when the public needs it], but a blessing [from God and man] is upon the head of him who sells it.
- *Matthew 10:8-10* - Heal the sick, cleanse the lepers, raise the dead, cast out devils: freely you have received, freely give. Provide neither gold, nor silver, nor brass in your purses, Nor money for your journey, neither two coats, neither shoes, nor yet staves: for the workman is worthy of his meat. …
- *Isaiah 55:1* - Come, all you who are thirsty, come to the waters; and you who have no money, come, buy and eat! Come, buy wine and milk without money and without cost.

- *Matthew 10:7* - As you go, proclaim this message: The kingdom of heaven has come near.

- *2 Corinthians 9:6-8* - The point is this: whoever sows sparingly will also reap sparingly, and whoever sows bountifully will also reap bountifully. Each one must give as he has decided in his heart, not reluctantly or under compulsion, for God loves a cheerful giver. And God is able to make all grace abound to you, so that having all sufficiency in all things at all times, you may abound in every good work.

- *Luke 6:38* - Give, and it will be given to you. Good measure, pressed down, shaken together, running over, will be put into your lap. For with the measure you use it will be measured back to you.

- *Hebrews 6:10-13* - For God is not unrighteous to forget your work and labor of love, which ye have shewed toward his name, in that ye have ministered to the saints, and do minister. And we desire that every one of you do shew the same diligence to the full assurance of hope unto the end: That ye be not slothful, but followers of them who through faith and patience inherit the promises.

  - God doesn't miss anything. He knows perfectly well all the love you've shown him by helping needy Christians, and that you keep at it. And now I want each of you to extend that same intensity toward a full–

bodied hope, and keep at it till the finish. Don't drag your feet. Be like those who stay the course with committed faith and then get everything promised to them. (The Message Version)

Supernatural Provision & Reaping:

There are seasons God will abundantly pour out his provision and blessings. We will experience, miracles and supernatural release. Blessings will come from unexpected sources, by God's ordained provision, or as the result of what we have sown in previous seasons. It is important to identify these seasons, and to expect and look for God to bless and open miraculous doors so you can acquire all He is releasing to you.

Testifying of God's supernatural provision is also important in this season as it encourages and opens up wells of supernatural provision in the lives of others. Discerning this season, will also assist in times where God is moving by His timing rather than ours. The reason He isn't answering could be because we are not in this season.

- ☐ *Exodus 12:2* -This month shall be for you the beginning of months. It shall be the first month of the year for you.
- ☐ *Philippians 4:19* - And my God will supply every need of yours according to his riches in glory in Christ Jesus.
- ☐ *Deuteronomy 8:18* - But remember the LORD your God is the one who makes you wealthy. He's confirming the promise which he swore to your ancestors. It's still in effect today.

- *Proverbs 10:22* - The blessing of the LORD, it maketh rich, and He adds no sorrow with it.
- *Proverbs 24:3-4* - Through wisdom is a house builded; and by understanding it is established: And by knowledge shall the chambers be filled with all precious and pleasant riches.
- *2 Corinthians 8:9* - For you know the grace of our Lord Jesus Christ, that, though he was rich. yet for your sakes He became poor, so that you through his poverty might be made rich.
- *2 Corinthians 9:10-11* -Now He that gives seed to the sower -gives you both bread for your food, and multiplies your seed sown, and increases the fruits of your righteousness;... so that you will be made rich in everything and in every way, which results in many thanksgivings to God.
- *Malachi 3:10* - Bring ye all the tithes into the storehouse, that there may be meat in mine house, and prove me now herewith, saith the LORD of hosts, if I will not open you the windows of heaven, and pour you out a blessing, that there shall not be room enough to receive it.
- *Matthew 6:33* - But seek you first the kingdom of God, and his righteousness; and all these things shall be added unto you.
- *Psalm 112:3* - Wealth and riches are in their houses, and their righteousness endures forever.

☐ *Proverbs 8:18* - With me are riches and honor, enduring wealth and prosperity.

☐ *Titus 1:3* - And at the proper time manifested in his word through the preaching with which I have been entrusted by the command of God our Savior;

☐ *Hosea 10:12* - Sow for yourselves righteousness; reap steadfast love; break up your fallow ground, for it is the time to seek the Lord, that he may come and rain righteousness upon you.

☐ *Song of Solomon 2:11-13* - For behold, the winter is past; the rain is over and gone. The flowers appear on the earth, the time of singing has come, and the voice of the turtledove is heard in our land. The fig tree ripens its figs, and the vines are in blossom; they give forth fragrance. Arise, my love, my beautiful one, and come away.

Relationship Building:

Have you been set apart for a time or even isolated so that God can build a greater intimate relationship with you? Is there a yearning in your heart that nothing earthly or that no person seems to fulfill? Has God closed the doors of anyone else being able to support, encourage, and empower you as He wants to be the ultimate source in your life for this season, or are you in a season of needing to be closed in with God to be empowered and prepared for a greater depth of destiny?

God enjoys time alone with us and will require seasons of being set apart unto Him. God will especially require this of single saints. He will draw singles unto Himself for a time of fellowship, relationship building, teaching, preparation, etc. Such seasons can feel lonely as often we initially pursue people and things rather than drawing unto the Lord or even seeing this as God's way as drawing us unto Him.

- *Psalms 37:4* - Delight yourself in the LORD and he will give you the desires of your
- heart.
- *James 4:8* - Draw near to God and He will draw near to you.
  Proverbs 8:33-35 Hear instruction, and be wise, and refuse it not. Blessed is the man that hears me, watching daily at my gates, waiting at the posts of my doors. For whoever finds me finds life, and shall obtain favor of the Lord.
- *Jeremiah 31:3* - The Lord appeared to him from far away. I have loved you with an everlasting love; therefore I have continued my faithfulness to you.
- *Isaiah 65:24* - Before they call I will answer; while they are yet speaking I will hear.
- *Isaiah 55:1-3* - Come, everyone who thirsts, come to the waters; and he who has no money, come, buy and eat! Come, buy wine and milk without money and without price. Why do you spend your money for that which is not bread, and your labor for that which does not satisfy? Listen diligently to me, and eat what is good,

and delight yourselves in rich food. Incline your ear, and come to me; hear, that your soul may live; and I will make with you an everlasting covenant, my steadfast, sure love for David.

- ☐ *Zephaniah 3:17* - The Lord your God is in your midst, a mighty one who will save; he will rejoice over you with gladness; he will quiet you by his love; he will exult over you with loud singing.
- ☐ *Jeremiah 33:3* - Call to me and I will answer you, and will tell you great and hidden things that you have not known.
- ☐ *John 15:4-6* - Abide in me, and I in you. As the branch cannot bear fruit by itself, unless it abides in the vine, neither can you, unless you abide in me. I am the vine; you are the branches. Whoever abides in me and I in him, he it is that bears much fruit, for apart from me you can do nothing. If anyone does not abide in me he is thrown away like a branch and withers; and the branches are gathered, thrown into the fire, and burned.
- ☐ *1Corinthians 7:32* - But I would have you without carefulness. He that is unmarried careth for the things that belong to the Lord, how he may please the Lord:

Teaching His Sovereignty:
There are some seasons when we just learn that God is sovereign. That God is God and no matter what we pray, what we desire, what is occurring, God is in

control and He will intervene at His appointed time. Generally this season is to teach us to lean on God just because of who He is - not for what He does, what He will do, or what He has done. But simply because of who He is as our Lord, and who He is as the creator of the entire universe. This season can be challenging as we strive to understand what we know about God, what He has spoken and promised, versus Him simply operating in the existence of who He is. The most awesome fact about God being sovereign is that, eventually, who He is begins to manifests in our lives in due time. God cannot be who He is and not bless His people. If we hold true to this fact, it will give us great peace during seasons of God's sovereignty.

- ☐ **Deuteronomy 32:39** - See now that I, even I, am he, and there is no god beside me; I kill and I make alive; I wound and I heal; and there is none that can deliver out of my hand.

- ☐ **Proverbs 16:33** - The lot is cast into the lap, but its every decision is from the Lord.

- ☐ **Job 12:13-14** - With God are wisdom and might; he has counsel and understanding. If he tears down, none can rebuild; if he shuts a man in, none can open.

- ☐ **2Chronicles 20:6** - And said, "O Lord, God of our fathers, are you not God in heaven? You rule over all the kingdoms of the nations. In your hand are power and might, so that none is able to withstand you.

- ☐ **Psalm 115:3** - Our God is in the heavens; he
- ☐ does all that he pleases.

Job 23:13 - But he is unchangeable, and who can turn him back? What he desires, that he does.

☐ *Lamentations 3:37* - Who has spoken and it came to pass, unless the Lord has commanded it?

Delivering & Healing

During seasons of deliverance and healing, God will seek to free us from deep hurts, offenses, past issues, soul ties, generational strongholds, curses, evil decrees, and judgments. In this season, God may reveal past unpleasant experiences, family secrets, unconscious and hidden offenses, shameful and guilty bondages. This season will hurt at times, but as God deeply cleanses, the deliverance and healing will produce great joy and freedom. This season can be coupled with unpleasant dreams of past experiences and flashbacks. God may constantly bring character flaws or offenses before you in an effort to expose what He desires to heal. There will even be instances where you will realize that you are angry at God for experiences you have endured. This will be a time of being honest before God, while asking for forgiveness, releasing forgiveness, renouncing demonic strongholds, and soaking in the deliverance and healing power of the Holy Spirit. Though deliverance and healing should be continual in every season, specific seasons of deliverance and healing is necessary for allowing God to deal with deep rooted issues that hinder destiny. Submitting to these seasons, makes them easier to get through as resisting can prolong the process to healthiness.

47

☐ *Psalms 51:6-8* - Behold, you desire truth in the inward parts: and in the hidden part you shall make me to know wisdom. Purge me with hyssop, and I shall be clean: wash me, and I shall be whiter than snow. Make me to hear joy and gladness; that the bones which you have broken may rejoice.

☐ *Psalm 51:2* - Wash away all my iniquity and

☐ cleanse me from my sin.

Ezekiel 36:25 - I will sprinkle clean water on you, and you will be clean; I will cleanse you from all your impurities and from all your idols.

☐ *Hebrews 10:22* - Let us draw near to God with a sincere heart in full assurance of faith, having our hearts sprinkled to cleanse us from a guilty conscience and having our bodies washed with pure water

☐ *Micah 7:19* - He will have compassion upon us; he will subdue our iniquities; and thou wilt cast all their sins into the depths of the sea.

☐ *Isaiah 1:18* - Come now, and let us reason together, saith the LORD: though your sins be as scarlet, they shall be as white as snow; though they be red like crimson, they shall be as wool.

☐ *Joel 2:12-13* - Therefore also now, saith the LORD, turn ye even to me with all your heart, and with fasting, and with weeping, and with mourning: And rend your heart, and not your garments, and turn unto the LORD your God: for he is gracious and merciful, slow to anger,

48

and of great kindness, and repenteth him of the evil.

☐ ***Psalms 103:2-4*** - Bless the LORD, O my soul, and forget not all his benefits: Who forgiveth all thine iniquities; who healeth all thy diseases; Who redeemeth thy life from destruction; who crowneth thee with loving kindness and tender mercies.

Spiritual Application:

Has the Holy Spirit had you in a time of learning and now He has released you to apply what you have learned? You keep trying to learn and it starts to feel as if you are becoming stagnant or that you want to spiritually regurgitate, because you do not have any spiritual room to take in more? This is probably because it is time to apply what you have feasted upon.

Often in this season, the things that are preached and studied, just appear mediocre or difficult for us to comprehend. We start to feel frustrated because we equate our frustrations or challenges to desiring or needing more of God, when it really is a season of applying so that we literally become what we have ingested.

> ***Psalms 34:8*** *Oh, taste and see that the Lord is good; Blessed is the man who trusts in Him!*

Once we have tasted of knowledge, we have obtained that revelation. However, the only way to see His goodness in that revelation is to actually apply that knowledge to our lives and situations. Without actually applying it, that knowledge is just revelation held in our spirits. Hiding information in our hearts is definitely biblical as **Psalms 119:11** says, *"Thy word have I hid in mine heart, that I might not sin against thee."* However, there is a season where that word needs to be exposed and applied to our lives.

- *Philippians 4:9* - Whatever you have learned or received or heard from me, or seen in me--put it into practice. And the God of peace will be with you.

- Those things, which you have both learned, and received, and heard, and seen in me, do: and the God of peace shall be with you (KJV).

Knowing The Reasons For Life Challenges

There are various reasons for life challenges:

o To teach you something o Build a gift or character in you o Resistance from the enemy against destiny

o A shift in destiny alignment

o This path is necessary to further progress to destiny

o Demonic warfare

o Disobedience to God

o Obedience to God

o Personal choices or actions have caused challenges

Once you have identified the reason, then you can close any unnecessary doors or entryways to unnecessary warfare.

You can also effectively identify a plan to align with what God is doing or counterattack what the enemy is doing.

Questions For Spiritual Exploration:

1. Ask God what is the reason for your life challenges?

2. Pray into what He tells you and close any doors or portals to unnecessary warfare. Also open any doors that need to be open for you to progress forward in Him.

3. Cleanse yourself of any frustration that maybe preventing you from further aligning with His plan in this season.

4. Ask God for His strategy of counterattack against the enemy and what your role is in this trial. Implement what God speaks to you.

Retreating The Soul

There are times in the journey where it is not the season to rest, but continual respite is needed to remain refreshed and rejuvenated in the assignment.

Psalms 23:1-3 KJV
The Lord is my shepherd; I shall not want. He maketh me to lie down in green pastures: he leadeth me beside the still waters. He restoreth my soul: he leadeth me in the paths of righteousness for his name's sake.

Amplified
THE LORD is my Shepherd [to feed, guide, and shield me], I shall not lack. He makes me lie down in [fresh, tender] green pastures; He leads me beside the still and restful waters. He refreshes and restores my life (myself); He leads me in the paths of righteousness [uprightness and right standing with Him – not for my earning it, but] for His name's sake.

The Message:
God, my shepherd! I don't need a thing. You have bedded me down in lush meadows, you find me quiet pools to drink from. True to your word, you let me catch my breath and send me in the right direction.

Restoreth is *Sub* in the Hebrew and means:

1. To turn back (hence, away), (not necessarily with the idea of return to the starting point); generally to retreat (retreat the soul);

2. Pull in again, put (again, up again), recall, recover, refresh, relieve, render (again),

3. Requite, pay recompense, rescue, restore, retrieve, (cause to, make to) return, reverse, refresh, reward, revoke

4. Send back, set again, slide back, to still, take back (off), (cause to, make to) turn (again, self again, away, back, back again, backward, bring home again.

Restoring from
- o dying of human relations
- o of spiritual relations
- o to turn back (from God)

To retreat the soul

1. The forced or strategic withdrawal of an army or an armed force before an enemy, or the withdrawing of a naval force from action.

2. The act of withdrawing, as into safety or privacy; retirement; seclusion.

3. A place of refuge, seclusion, or privacy:

4. An asylum, as for the insane.

5. A retirement or a period of retirement for religious exercises and meditation.

Though we are not in a place of rest, it is important to take moments to retreat the soul:

Often when we get to this place of needing a refreshing, we try to do it ourselves. But the scriptures let us know that God has to lead us in this refreshing.

- o He maketh me to lie down in green pastures
- o He leadeth me beside the still waters
- o He restoreth my soul
- o He leadeth me in the paths of righteousness for his name's sake

Leadeth is *Nathal* and means to:
1. To run with a sparkle, i.e. flow, to conduct, to protect, sustain: — carry, feed, guide
2. To lead to a watering- place or station and cause to rest there
3. To lead or bring to a station or goal to lead,
4. Guide, to give rest to, to refresh (with food)
5. To lead on to journey by stations

God knows where the green pastures and the still waters are in your journey. He knows how to get you to that respite place of empowerment needed to continue your journey.

There are however, two keys to receiving the green pastures and the watering.

- o First you have to lie down (crouch/surrender inside the protection of God)

- o Then you have to get still (repose and get quiet)

These are the postured places where He can lead you. In **Matthew 26:3645**, as Jesus was in the garden of Gethsemane, He told the disciples that His soul was exceedingly sorrowful and vexed unto death and to tarry with Him, while He went a little further into the garden (into the pastures) to pray.

The word says Jesus went in and fell on
His face in prayer.
Verse 39

> *And he went a little further, and fell on his face, and prayed, saying, O my Father, if it be possible, let this cup pass from me: nevertheless not as I will, but as thou wilt.*

When he came to check on the disciples they were asleep and he said: *Verse 40*

> *What, could ye not watch with me one hour? Watch and pray, that ye enter not into temptation: the spirit indeed is willing, but the flesh is weak.*

The Message

> *When he came back to his disciples, he found them sound asleep. He said to Peter, "Can't you stick it out with me a single hour? Stay alert; be in prayer so you don't wander into temptation without even knowing you're in danger. There is a part of you that is eager, ready for anything in God. But there's another part that's as lazy as an old dog sleeping by the fire."*

When He was saying stay alert, He was saying to stay in prayer. He left again and was still seeking God for restoration of his soul, "*O my Father, if this cup may not pass away from me, except I drink it, thy will be done.*" When Jesus came back at this time, they were sleep again. He went away a third time and prayed the same word. Jesus was on a heavy assignment - a destiny assignment. Jesus took a moment in the journey to get His soul renewed and was demonstrating to the disciples how to receive the green pastures and the still waters in the midst of a heavy assignment.

Many of us feel drained and heavy at times, and though our spirits are eager to continue with God, we just want to naturally sleep or spiritually give into being slothful. But during these seasons, it is important to retreat in God, thus continuing in the momentum with God. Jesus received restoration of His soul in God as He progressed forward into his destiny assignment. When Jesus finally returned to the disciples He said:

> *Then cometh he to his disciples, and saith unto them, Sleep on now, and take your rest: behold, the hour is at hand, and the Son of man is betrayed into the hands of sinners. Rise, let us be going: behold, he is at hand that doth betray me.*

Each time Jesus went into the pastures of quiet, He was empowered in his journey.

He went from:

57

- Take this cup: *let this cup pass from me: nevertheless not as I will, but as thou wilt.*
- To help me drink this cup: *O my Father, if this cup may not pass away from me, except I drink it, thy will be done.*
- To let us walk it out: *Sleep on now, and take your rest: behold, the hour is at hand... Rise, let us be going.*

In this time of proper posture Jesus went from *"please deliver me"* to *"it is on and poppin."*

I want to note that Jesus took an hour. He told the disciples, can you not pray with me for one hour. This is not a season of rest but a moment of refreshing. We must refresh with the mindset of continuing on in the full vision that is before us. Jesus was honest with God about the fact that He really was hesitant about going on, and would rather be rescued, but He also knew that progression was inevitable. He thus did not take a detour or break from his assignment. He took respite in God and therefore, continued with God.

Steps For Retreating The Soul

1. Set aside time to focus on just refreshing in God. Do not focus on anything but this and the vision/assignment at hand.

2. If you are in a heavy battle or on a serious destiny assignment, have others intercede for you while you pray and journeying. Jesus truly just wanted the encouragement of knowing others were with Him, and fortified in the will of God for his life. This is always encouraging.

3. Lie down in green pastures (crouch/surrender inside the protection of God), and get still in his waters (repose and get quiet). Go to a serene place where you can sit or lie before Jesus.

4. Declare and soak (spend time actually soaking and absorbing God's presence) in the consumption of God's replenishment (green pastures), and refreshment of his living waters (still waters).

    a. The Hebrew word for green is "*dese*" and means *a sprout, herb, green, grass, new grass, green herb, vegetation, young.* Green represents prosperity and replenishment.

    b. The Hebrew word for waters is "*Maiym*" and means *juice, water springs, washing, watercourse, flood, water flood, watering.*

Waters represent refreshment and renewal.

5. Be honest with the Lord regarding all your insecurities, fears, hesitancies, and heaviness with having to carry out the vision that is before you.

6. Be conscious in receiving God's refreshment, as He may not take the cup, but His pastures and waters will empower you to press forward.

7. Keep going back for respite as much as you need. Take daily retreats or short retreats throughout the day if nothing but five minutes. Take time to go inside God, even just within yourself and replenish.

8. Keep asking others to support as Jesus did with the disciples. Often you are the one carrying the mantle of the vision so your strength and sustaining power is greater than those around you. Therefore, do not get discouraged if others cannot tarry with you. Share wisdom with them as Jesus did. Encourage them to stay alert while you remain focused on the ultimate goal.

9. And as you keep retreating in God and pursue support, make sure you keep pressing forward in the momentum of God until the assignment is fulfilled. STAY THE COURSE WITH GOD!

Retreating In The Journey Decree!

1. One thing I ask of the LORD, this is what I seek: that I may dwell in the house of You LORD all the days of my life, to gaze upon the beauty of the LORD and to seek Him in his temple… My heart pursues in a decree, 'Seek God's face!' Your face, Lord, I seek." (Psalm 27:4, 8)

2. For as the deer pants for streams of water, so my soul pants for You, O God. My soul thirsts for God, for the living God. I shift into my meeting place with God?" (Psalm 42:1-2)

3. Awake, my soul! Awake, harp and lyre! I will awaken the dawn. I will praise You, O Lord, among the nations; I will sing of You among the peoples. For great is Your love, reaching to the heavens; Your faithfulness reaches to the skies. (Psalm 57:8-10)

4. I am thanking You, God, out loud in the streets, singing Your praises in town and country. The deeper Your love, the higher it goes; every cloud is a flag to Your faithfulness. Soar high in the skies, O God! Cover the whole earth with your glory! (Verse 9-11 The Message Version)

5. Find rest, O my soul, in God alone; my hope comes from You Lord. You alone are my rock and my salvation; You are my fortress, I will not be shaken. My salvation and my honor depend on You God; You are my mighty rock, my refuge. I trust in You at all times, O people; pour out your hearts to Him, for God is our refuge. (Psalm 62:5-8

6. God, the one and only--I'll wait as long as he says. Everything I hope for comes from Him, so why not? He's solid rock under my feet, breathing room for my soul, An impregnable castle: I am set for life. My help and glory are in God--granite-strength and safe-harbor-God- - So trust Him absolutely, people; lay your lives on the line for Him. God is a safe place to be. (Verse 5-8, The Message Version)

7. O God, you are my God, earnestly I seek You; my soul thirsts for You, my body longs for You, in a dry and weary land where there is no water. I have seen You in the sanctuary and beheld Your power and Your glory. Because Your love is better than life, my lips will glorify You. I will praise You as long as I live, and in Your name I will lift up my hands. My soul will be satisfied as with the richest of foods; with singing lips my mouth will praise You. On my bed I remember You; I think of You through the watches of the night. Because You are my
help, I sing in the shadow of Your wings. My soul clings to You; Your right hand upholds me (Psalm 63:1-8).

8. God--You're my God! I can't get enough of You! I've worked up such hunger and thirst for God, traveling across dry and weary deserts. So here I am in the place of worship, eyes open, drinking in Your strength and glory. In Your generous love I am really living at last! My lips brim praises like fountains. I bless You every time I take a breath;

62

My arms wave like banners of praise to You.
(Verses 1-8, The Message)

9. Whom have I in heaven but You? And earth has nothing I desire besides You. My flesh and my heart may fail, but God is the strength of my heart and my portion forever (Psalm 73:25-26)

10. Whom do I have in heaven but You? I desire no one but You on earth. My flesh and my heart may grow weak, but You God always protects my heart and gives me stability. (Verse 25-26, NET Version)

11. How lovely is Your dwelling place, O Lord Almighty! My soul yearns, even faints, for the courts of the LORD; my heart and my flesh cry out for the living God. Even the sparrow has found a home, and the swallow a nest for herself, where she may have her young — a place near your altar, O LORD Almighty, my King and my God. Blessed am I because I dwell in Your house; I am forever praising You (Psalms 84:1-4).

12. Better is one day in Your courts Lord than a thousand elsewhere; I would rather be a doorkeeper in the house of my God than dwell in the tents of the wicked. (Psalm 84:10)

13. My heart is steadfast, O God; I will sing and make music with all my soul. (Psalm 108:1)

14. My soul is consumed with longing for Your laws at all times…My soul faints with longing for Your salvation" (Psalm 119:20, 81).

15. I spread out my hands to You; my soul thirsts for You like a parched land. (Psalm 143:6)

16. I need more than bread for their life; I must feed on every word of God. (Matthew 4:4, NLT)

17. I am blessed when I have worked up a good appetite for God. God you are food and drink. The best meal I have ever eaten (Matthew 5:6, The Message Version).

18. Like Jesus, my food, is to do the will of God who sends me forth and to finish His works. (John 4:34)

19. For the bread of God is He who comes down from heaven and gives life to the world. Even as Jesus declared that He is the bread of life, I come to Him and feast and therefore, I am never hungry (John 6:33-35).

20. As I feast inside the respite of Jesus, my glory is fresh in me, and my bow is renewed in my hand (Job 29:20).

Seasons of Character Building

The character of God is very complex, as just when we think we understand Him, He presents another avenue of Himself that lets us know we are yet learning His nature and His image. Within seasons, God will allow situations to help instill and build His character and fruit in us. When God is building His character, He is exposing and maturing the image of Himself that He created us to be.

> **Genesis 1:27**
> *So God created man in his own image, in the image of God created he him; male and female created he them.*

<u>*Image* is *Selem* in Hebrew and means:</u>

1. Illusion, resemblance, hence, a representative figure, especially an idol: — likeness.
2. representation; counterpart

<u>Synonyms of the word *"image"* from Dictionary.com</u>

carbon copy	equal	model
carved	form	photocopy
figure	icon	photograph
copy	illustration	picture
dead ringer	likeness	portrait
double	match	reflection

What reasons does God desire us to mature and be the very photocopy/reflection of His character?

> ### 2Corinthians 10:3-6
> *For though we walk in the flesh, we do not war after the flesh: (For the weapons of our warfare are not carnal, but mighty through God to the pulling down of strong holds;) Casting down imaginations, and every high thing that exalteth itself against the knowledge of God, and bringing into captivity every thought to the obedience of Christ; And having in a readiness to revenge all disobedience, when your obedience is fulfilled.*
>
> *The Message Version*
> *The world is unprincipled. It's dog-eat-dog out there! The world doesn't fight fair. But we don't live or fight our battles that way — never have and never will. **The tools of our trade** aren't for marketing or manipulation, but they are for demolishing that entire massively corrupt culture. We use our powerful God-tools for smashing warped philosophies, tearing down barriers erected against the truth of God, fitting every loose thought and emotion and impulse into the structure of life shaped by Christ. Our tools are ready at hand for clearing the ground of every obstruction and building lives of obedience into maturity.*

The reason God's character is so important is that it serves as a weapon, a
"tool of our trade," in being able to cast down anything that is contrary to Him and His desire for our lives.

Such knowledge can only come with us being rooted and grounded in God's character and fruit, and distinctly displaying His nature with maturity and confident authority.

There are character traits that belong to God alone. For example: Him being sovereign, eternal, the only God, infinite, supreme, and all knowing. However, there are those traits to which we share in the likeness of His image. There is no way to list all of God's characteristics. I will just provide a list and encourage you to study His character more in detail in your personal time as this study is essential for identifying what trait He may be maturing in you.

Character Traits Of God

Alert Mark 14:28
Attentive Hebrews 2:1
Available Philemon 2:20
Bold Acts 4:29
Compassionate 1John 3:17
Confident 2Timothy 1:7
Content 1Timothy 6:8
Creative Ephesians 2:10
Dependable Isaiah 55:11
Determined 2Timothy 4:7-8
Diligent Colossians 3:23

Gracious Nehemiah 9:17
Grateful 1Corinthians 4:7
Good 2Chronicles 7:3
Holy 1Peter 1:16
Hospitable Hebrew 13:2
Humility James 4:6
Initiating Romans 12:21
Jealous Exodus 34:14
Joyful Proverbs 15:13
Just Micah 6:8
Kind Isaiah 54:8
Loving 1Corinthians 13
Loyal John 15:13
Meek Psalms 62:5
Merciful 2Samuel 24:14
Obedient 2Corinthians 10:5
Orderly 1Corinthians 14:40

Discerning 1Samuel 16:7
Discrete Proverbs 22:3
Empowering Philippians 4:13
Enduring Galatians 6:9
Enthusiastic 1Thessalonians 5-15-16
Fathering 1Corinthians 8:6
Faithful Hebrews 11:1
Flexible Colossians 3:2
Forgiving Ephesians 4:32
Generous 2Corinthians 9:6
Gentle 1Thessalonians 2:7
Persuasive 2Timothy 2:24
Punctual Ecclesiastes 3:1
Pure Titus 1:15
Reconciler 2Corinthians 5:18
Resourceful Luke 16:10
Responsible Romans 14:12
Rewarding Hebrews 6:10
Righteous Job 37:23
Secure John 6:27
Self-controlled Galatians 5:24-25
Sensitive Romans 12:15
Sincere 1Peter 1:22
Sovereign Isaiah 14:27
Truthful Ephesians 4:25
Wise Proverbs 9:10
Worshipper Zephaniah 3:17
Wrath Psalms 7:11

Is God maturing His character in you? If so, are you submitting to the process of character building? Such a season will test your emotions, your flesh, and will cause great humility in times where you will want to retaliate, defend yourself, or assert righteous justice. Yet, God maybe requiring you to be the better person and hold your peace as doing so will establish in you a greater weight of glory.

- *1 Peter 5:6-7* - Humble yourselves therefore under the mighty hand of God, that he may exalt you in due time: casting all your care upon him; for he careth for you.
- *James 1:2-4* - My brethren, count it all joy when you fall into various trials, knowing that the testing of your faith produces patience. But let patience have its perfect work, that you may be perfect and complete, lacking nothing.
- *Romans 12:2* - Do not conform any longer to the pattern of this world, but be transformed by the renewing of your mind. Then you will

be able to test and approve what God's will is — his good, pleasing and perfect will.

- ☐ *1Thessalonians 1:3* - We remember before our God and Father your work produced by faith, your labor prompted by love, and your endurance inspired by hope in our Lord Jesus Christ.

- ☐ *2 Corinthians 3:18* - But we all, with unveiled face, beholding as in a mirror the glory of the Lord, are being transformed into the same image from glory to glory, just as by the Spirit of the Lord.

Character Building That Product God's Fruit:

The word tells us that we should know if something or someone is of God by their fruit. This is because the fruit of God is the manifestation of His character. If one is manifesting God's fruit then it is likely that he or she possess His character.

Matthew 16:16-21

> *Ye shall know them by their fruits. Do men gather grapes of thorns, or figs of thistles? Even so every good tree bringeth forth good fruit; but a corrupt tree bringeth forth evil fruit.*

> *A good tree cannot bring forth evil fruit, neither can a corrupt tree bring forth good fruit. Every tree that bringeth not forth good fruit is hewn down, and cast into the fire.*

> *Wherefore by their fruits ye shall know them. Not everyone that saith unto me, Lord, Lord, shall enter*

70

into the kingdom of heaven; but he that doeth the
will of my Father which is in heaven.

Luke 6:43-45
A good tree cannot have bad fruit. A bad tree cannot
have good fruit. For every tree is known by its own
fruit. Men do not gather figs from thorns. They do
not gather grapes from thistles. Good comes from a
good man because of the riches he has in his heart.
Sin comes from a sinful man because of the sin he
has in his heart. The mouth speaks of what the heart
is full of.

Proverbs 20:11
Even small children are known by their actions, so
is their conduct really pure and upright?

Matthew 12:33
Make a tree good and its fruit will be good, or make
a tree bad and its fruit will be bad, for a tree is
recognized by its fruit.

The fruit of the spirit is found in *Galatians 5:22-25:*

But the fruit of the Spirit is love, joy, peace,
longsuffering, gentleness, goodness, faith,
Meekness, temperance: against such there is no law.
And they that are Christ's have crucified the flesh
with the affections and lusts. If we live in the
Spirit, let us also walk in the Spirit.

The Amplified Version
But the fruit of the [Holy] Spirit [the work which
His presence within accomplishes] is love, joy

*(gladness), peace, patience (an even temper,
forbearance), kindness, goodness (benevolence),
faithfulness, gentleness (meekness, humility), self-
control (self-restraint, continence). Against such
things there is no law [[f]that can bring a charge].*

*And those who belong to Christ Jesus (the Messiah)
have crucified the flesh (the godless human nature)
with its passions and appetites and desires. If we
live by the [Holy] Spirit, let us also walk by the
Spirit. [If by the Holy Spirit [g]we have our life in
God, let us go forward [h]walking in line, our
conduct controlled by the Spirit.]*

As God builds your character, He will be looking for
specific fruit that demonstrates what is being revealed
and matured within you. This is the purpose of the
season of character building. It is to assist you with
properly applying the fruit of the character that is
being cultivated. It is also important to note that the
word *fruit* is singular in this scripture; therefore, when
God desires us to apply a specific fruit, such as love,
He is requiring that we are able to present every
characteristic of that fruit. Not just some portions of
that fruit, but every part and form of it. This is where
the season can be challenging. The fruit God is
maturing in us has to be pure and unadulterated. It
cannot be conditional or applied when we desire. It
has to be sovereign just like God, and contingent only
at His leading. Let us explore some of the fruit in
Galatians in hopes of further exploring this revelation.
Fruit of Love:

1Corinthians 13:4-7

Love suffers long and is kind; love does not envy; love does not parade itself, is not puffed up; does not behave rudely, does not seek its own, is not provoked, thinks no evil; does not rejoice in iniquity, but rejoices in the truth; bears all things, believes all things, hopes all things, endures all things.

In this passage of scripture we are shown the fruit of love. If God is maturing love in you, He will be requiring you to be able to manifest every characteristic of that fruit. You cannot say you love but be envious or puffed up. The season of love will produce testing and trial to purge you of the negative attributes that prevent you from exhibiting pure love. You may have to humble yourself in situations where you feel you should display conditional love or withhold your love. Yet God will require you to love unconditionally.

☐ *1 Peter 4:8* - And above all things have fervent charity among yourselves: for charity shall cover the multitude of sins.

☐ *John 13:34-35* -A new command I give you: Love one another. As I have loved you, so you must love one another. By this all men will know that you are my disciples, if you love one another.

Fruit of Long Suffering/Patience:

Long Suffering is *Makrothymia* in the Greek and means:

1. Longanimity (enduring hardship, injuries, or offense), forbearance or fortitude
2. Patience, endurance, constancy, steadfastness, perseverance forbearance,
3. Slowness in avenging wrongs
4. To be longsuffering, slow to anger, slow to punish

It essentially means to exude enduring patience in love despite obstacles and trials.

Colossians 1:11-12 The Amplified

[We pray] that you may be invigorated and strengthened with all power according to the might of His glory, [to exercise] every kind of endurance and patience (perseverance and forbearance) with joy, Giving thanks to the Father, Who has qualified and made us fit to share the portion which is the inheritance of the saints (God's holy people) in the Light.

KJV

May you be strengthened with all power, according to his glorious might, for all endurance and patience with joy, Giving thanks unto the Father, which hath made us meet to be partakers of the inheritance of the saints in light:

Patience is *Hypomone* in the Greek and means:

1. cheerful (or hopeful) endurance, constancy: — enduring, patience, patient continuance (waiting).
2. steadfastness, constancy

3. endurance in the NT the characteristic of a man who is not swerved from his deliberate purpose and his loyalty to faith and piety by even the greatest trials and sufferings patiently, and steadfastly,

4. sustaining, perseverance

Whewww!!! To that definition! When we are being matured in patience we do not feel cheerful, as often we feel anxious, frustrated, and are challenged by having to wait. We never consider that God is working in us, such that we shift into a place of peace and even cheerful in the waiting. Who knew that being cheerful was an attribute of patience??? Jesus!!!

> ### *The Message Version*
> *We pray that you'll have the strength to stick it out over the long haul—not the grim strength of gritting your teeth but the glory-strength God gives. It is strength that endures the unendurable and spills over into joy, thanking the Father who makes us strong enough to take part in everything bright and beautiful that he has for us.*

Are you in a season where God is maturing your patience? What is hindering you from having peace and cheer as God has you endure life challenges?

- ☐ *1Timothy 1:16* - But I obtained mercy for the reason that in me, as the foremost [of sinners], Jesus Christ might show forth and display all His perfect long-suffering and patience for an example to [encourage] those who would thereafter believe on Him for [the gaining of] eternal life.

- *Psalm 40:1* - I waited patiently and expectantly for the Lord; and He inclined to me and heard my cry.

- *Colossians 3:12* - Clothe yourselves therefore, as God's own chosen ones (His own picked representatives), [who are] purified and holy and well-beloved [by God Himself, by putting on behavior marked by] tenderhearted pity and mercy, kind feeling, a lowly opinion of yourselves, gentle ways, [and] patience [which is tireless and longsuffering, and has the power to endure whatever comes, with good temper].

- *James 5:7* - Be patient, therefore, brothers, until the coming of the Lord. See how the farmer waits for the precious fruit of the earth, being patient about it, until it receives the early and the late rains.

Questions For Spiritual Exploration:

1. What is character?
2. How does God's image relate to his character?
3. What did you learn about the fruit of the spirit?
4. Study the remaining fruit in Galatians 5:22-23? Give three scriptures on each fruit. Study their meaning in "*Strong's Concordance,*" and note the revelation the Holy Spirit reveals to you.

Holy Spirit As A Friend

Please be aware that this self-exploration of the Holy Spirit will prick your spirit and will grieve you just a bit. The revelation definitely exposed and hurt me, but it is essential for cleansing past rejection and relationship cycles, embracing the Holy Spirit as our best friend, and really having a Spirit to Spirit relationship/friendship with Him rather than emotional and fleshly encounters with just His presence and character. So even now we thank you Lord for the self-exploration, exposure and the transformation.

The greatest app we have is the Holy Spirit.

> ### John 14-16-17 (The Amplified Version)
> *And I will ask the Father, and He will give you another Comforter*
> *(Counselor, Helper, Intercessor, Advocate, Strengthener, and Standby), that He may remain with you forever — The Spirit of Truth, Whom the world cannot receive (welcome, take to its heart), because it does not see Him or know and recognize Him. But you know and recognize Him, for He lives with you [constantly] and will be in you.*
>
> ### The Message Version
> *I will talk to the Father, and he'll provide you another Friend so that you will always have someone with you. This Friend is the Spirit of Truth. The godless world can't take him in because it doesn't have eyes to see him, doesn't know what*

to look for. But you know him already because he has been staying with you, and will even be in you!

God said that we tend to embrace the presence of the Holy Spirit, but have not received Him as our friend. This is huge within the body of Christ at present as praise and worship tends to be the center focus of Christendom.
People are being touched Sunday after Sunday by the presence of God. However, the experiences are making us feel good in our flesh and emotions, but we leave out of services unchanged because we lack a true Spirit to Spirit encounter. This is because we are just encountering the presence of the Holy Spirit, but lack true relationship with the Him.

God says when it comes to friendship we put everyone else in this position, while negating the Holy Spirit. We are always longing for someone else to comfort us, guide us, teach us, empower us, intercede for us, advocate for us. Though there is nothing wrong with desiring relationships and support, the Holy Spirit should be our best friend and should be the example of how we are to engage and govern every other relationship in our lives.

Jesus said that though the world would not be able to receive the Holy Spirit, we should be able to know and recognize Him, for He lives with us constantly and will be in us. That the world does not know what He looks like or what to look for, but we should know because He will be staying with us and will live in us.

Verse 17 (KJV)
Even the Spirit of truth; whom the world cannot receive, because it seeth him not, neither knoweth him: but ye know him; for he dwelleth with you, and shall be in you.

<u>*See*</u> is *Theoreo* in the Greek and means:

1. To be a spectator of, i. e. discern, (literally, figuratively (experience) or intensively (acknowledge) behold, consider, look on, perceive,

2. To be a spectator, look at, behold to view attentively, take a view of,

3. Survey to view mentally, consider to see to perceive with the eyes, to enjoy the presence of one

4. To discern, descry to ascertain, find out by seeing

<u>*Know*</u> is *Ginosko* in the Greek and means:

1. Allow, be aware (of), feel, (have) know (- ledge), perceived, be resolved, can speak, be sure, understand.

2. To learn to know, come to know, get a knowledge of, perceive, feel to become known

3. To understand to know Jewish idiom for sexual intercourse between a man and a woman, to become acquainted with

The world cannot discern the Holy Spirit but we should be able to. We should be able to know Him and become acquainted with Him as we would our spouse or someone we love. However, we acknowledge the Holy Spirit when we want His presence or the attributes of His character, such as His healing power or blessing; but we do not intensively behold Him in relationship as a loved one, as we would a spouse or friend. Though we are the ones who are to know Him, the Holy Spirit is constantly spurned and ostracized because of His position in our lives. Every time we dreadfully or lustfully wish for someone else or something else without initially drawing into the Holy Spirit, we reject, grieve and ostracized the Holy Spirit. For it is as if the one gift Jesus left to comfort us and be with us forever, we reject over and over and over and over again.

Verse 18(KJV)
I will not leave you comfortless: I will come to you.

Jesus obviously knew there would be lonely days. Days where others would forsake us; days where we would feel exposed, misunderstood, rejected, betrayed, uncertain, grieved; days where our spouses and friends would not be sufficient comfort for us; days where only relationship with Him would fulfill us.

Psalms 27:10
When my father and my mother forsake me, then the LORD will take me up.

Isaiah 49:15
Can a mother forget the baby at her breast and have no compassion on the child she has borne? Though she may forget, I will not forget you!

John 9:35

Jesus heard that they had cast him out; and when he had found him, he said unto him, Dost thou believe on the Son of God?

John 16:32

Behold, the hour cometh, yea, is now come, that ye shall be scattered, every man to his own, and shall leave me alone: and yet I am not alone, because the Father is with me.

2Timothy 4:16

At my first answer no man stood with me, but all men forsook me: I pray God that it may not be laid to their charge.

Jesus made sure we were comforted even when it appeared that no comfort was available or even possible. And more importantly, the gift He left us in the Holy Spirit would be able to speak truth to us, so that we could be empowered in the lowliest of times.

Verse 17 (KJV)

Even the Spirit of truth; whom the world cannot receive, because it seeth him not, neither knoweth him: but ye know him; for he dwelleth with you, and shall be in you.

Truth is *Aletheia* in the Greek and means:

1. Truth, truly, true, verity
2. Objectively what is true in any matter under consideration truly, in truth, according to truth of a truth, in reality, in fact

3. Certainly what is true in things appertaining to God and the duties of man, moral and religious truth in the greatest latitude the true notions of God which are open to human reason without his supernatural intervention

4. the truth as taught in the Christian religion, respecting God and the execution of his purposes through Christ, and respecting the duties of man, opposing alike to the superstitions of the Gentiles and the inventions of the Jews, and the corrupt opinions and precepts of false teachers even among Christians subjectively

5. Truth as a personal excellence that candor of mind which is free from affection, pretense, simulation, falsehood, deceit

The Holy Spirit was sent as a comforting friend of truth so we would not be deceived by the lies of the enemy. The lies that we are not loved, cared for, are lonely, helpless, purposeless, etc.

> *John 14:26*
> *But the Advocate, the Holy Spirit, whom the Father will send in my name, will teach you all things and will remind you of everything I have said to you.*

> *John 15:26*
> *When the Advocate comes, whom I will send to you from the Father--the*
> *Spirit of truth who goes out from the Father--he will testify about me.*

John 16:7

But very truly I tell you, it is for your good that I am going away. Unless I go away, the Advocate will not come to you; but if I go, I will send him to you

Romans 8:26

In the same way, the Spirit helps us in our weakness. We do not know what we ought to pray for, but the Spirit himself intercedes for us through wordless groans.

Holy Spirit Exploration

o   Explore times from childhood until now when you have sought people instead of the Holy Spirit. Ask the Holy Spirit how it made Him feel and repent for your actions. Spend time reconciling with the Holy Spirit as comforter and friend. Repent and cleanse yourself of any cycles and demonic strongholds of seeking people and being driven in being fulfilled by others rather than God.

o   Explore times from childhood until now where you gave into loneliness, depression, suicidal thoughts, etc., because you wanted someone to be there for you or desired something, yet did not draw into the Holy Spirit. Ask the Holy Spirit where He was during these experiences? Ask the Holy Spirit how your actions made Him feel? Spend time repenting and reconnecting to the Holy Spirit as comforter and friend.

Spend time breaking and falling out of agreement with those cycles and shifting your focus to drawing into the Holy Spirit from this day forward.

o Spend time from this day forward building a relationship with the Holy Spirit: Here are some suggestions for doing that: o Commune with the Holy Spirit daily and all throughout the day like you would a friend.

o Ask the Holy Spirit His likes and dislikes and repent quickly when you grieve the Holy Spirit (Study Ephesians 4:30, Matthew 12:31-
32), Hebrews 10:26-29, Acts 5:3, Acts 7:51) o Ask the Holy Spirit to teach you His ways and how to be in relationship with Him, and implement what He says.

o Do not move on a matter without the voice of the Holy Spirit. Get
His counsel and direction before making a decision o Include the Holy Spirit when you are praying and studying your word. Ask Him what and who He wants you to pray for, how you should spend your prayer time (soak, warfare, intercession, decreeing, etc.). Ask Him what you should study and to give you revelation of what you are studying.

o Ask Him to help you discern between truth and deceit, especially when you are in seasons of warfare, stressed, weary, experiencing a challenging situation, are overly emotional, feeling lonely or ostracized, etc.

o When you find yourself obsessed or drawn more to a person or thing repent quickly and reconnect to the Holy Spirit.

o When you start to feel lonely, depressed, overly emotional, immediately seek comfort and love from the Holy Spirit.

o Read the Book *"Good Morning Holy Spirit"* by Benny Hinn and *"The Shack"* by William P. Young (study other books, sermons, teachings, on the Holy Spirit and ask Him to make what you study a lifestyle in your life).

o Ask the Holy Spirit for His nature. You do this by asking the Holy Spirit how to discern and operate in His gifts, character, and fruit, and to provide opportunities for you to grow and mature in each area.

o Gifts of the Spirit (Study 1Corinthians 12, Isaiah 11:2-3, Ephesians 4:11--16)

o Character of the Holy Spirit (Study John 3:1-5, 1Corinthians 12,

Ephesians 1:13–14; 5:18)

o Fruit of the spirit(Study Galatians 5:22-23)

o Ask the Holy Spirit to teach you how to have Spirit to Spirit encounters with Him where you are not just experiencing His presence, but are truly being empowered, enlightened, rejuvenated, and transformed by His presence, His voice, and your relationship with Him. As the Holy Spirit is teaching you Spirit to Spirit encounters:

o Be obedient to what the Holy Spirit speaks

o Staying in the process of deliverance, healing and maturation until the Holy Spirit gives you further direction.   Do not abort the process by giving into emotions, frustration, or implementing your own plans.

> o   Do not expect the Holy Spirit to always perform for you. If He does not speak or you do not hear Him, do not assume that He is not their or working. Though God is touched by feelings, He is not a feeling. So we are not going to always feel Him. God is sovereign and He operates by the truth and Spirit of who He is. We should know He is with us and that He is active in the relationship with us even when He is silent, and even when our flesh and emotions are not feeling His tangible presence.
>
> *God is touched by our feelings so we can boldly approach Him and know that He is*

willing to help us regardless to whether He says or does anything.

Hebrews 4:14-16
Seeing then that we have a great high priest, that is passed into the heavens, Jesus the Son of God, let us hold fast our profession. For we have not an high priest which cannot be touched with the feeling of our infirmities; but was in all points tempted like as we are, yet without sin. Let us therefore come boldly unto the throne of grace, that we may obtain mercy, and find grace to help in time of need.

Learn to walk in the Spirit and not by emotions and flesh.
Galatians 5:16-25
This I say then, Walk in the Spirit, and ye shall not fulfill the lust of the flesh. For the flesh lusteth against the Spirit, and the Spirit against the flesh: and these are contrary the one to the other: so that ye cannot do the things that ye would.

But if ye be led of the Spirit, ye are not under the law. Now the works of the flesh are manifest, which are these; Adultery, fornication, uncleanness, lasciviousness, Idolatry, witchcraft, hatred, variance, emulations, wrath, strife, seditions, heresies, Envyings, murders, drunkenness, revellings, and such like: of the which I tell you before, as I have also told you in time past, that they which do such things shall not inherit the kingdom of God.

But the fruit of the Spirit is love, joy, peace, longsuffering, gentleness, goodness, faith, Meekness, temperance: against such there is no law. And they that are Christ's have crucified the flesh with the affections and lusts. If we live in the Spirit, let us also walk in the Spirit.

Spirit to Spirit worship, worships God for who He is and what His word says and not according to feeling, or what God is doing or not doing. This level of worship is sovereign as God is sovereign. It is being in relationship with God simply because He is God and because of the truth of His word. So even when we do not feel Him, hear Him, or when He isn't moving how we desire, we remain in connection with Him through the knowledge that He is always with us, He has a plan for us, and His plans and word for us is yes and Amen. They will not return void and they will come to pass as we grow and advance in our walk with Him.

John 4:23-24
But the hour cometh, and now is, when the true worshippers shall worship the Father in spirit and in truth: for the Father seeketh such to worship him. God is a Spirit: and they that worship him must worship him in spirit and in truth.

The Message Version

It's who you are and the way you live that count before God. Your worship must engage your spirit in the pursuit of truth. That's the kind of people the Father is out looking for: those who are simply and honestly themselves before him in their worship. God is sheer being itself— Spirit. Those who worship him must do it out of their very being, their spirits, their true selves, in adoration.

When we hang out with our friends, sometimes we do nothing. We just sit in a room and be with one another. As we pursue relationship with the Holy Spirit we have to do the same thing, while trusting that even when nothing is going on, we are building relationship by spending time, and God is right there in the midst of us. He is spending time just being with us.

Deuteronomy 31:8
It is the Lord who goes before you. He will be with you; he will not leave you or forsake you. Do not fear or be dismayed."

Deuteronomy 31:6
Be strong and courageous. Do not fear or be in dread of them, for it is the Lord your God who goes with you. He will not leave you or forsake you.

Micah 7:7

*But as for me, I will look to the Lord; I will wait
for the God of my salvation; my God will hear
me.*

Psalm 73:23-26

*Nevertheless, I am continually with you; you
hold my right hand. You guide me with your
counsel, and afterward you will receive me to
glory. Whom have I in heaven but you? And
there is nothing on earth that I desire besides
you. My flesh and my heart may fail, but God is
the strength of my heart and my portion forever.*

Zephaniah 3:17 (The Amplified Version)

*The Lord your God is in the midst of you, a
Mighty One, a Savior [Who saves]! He will
rejoice over you with joy; He will rest [in silent
satisfaction] and in His love He will be silent
and make no mention [of past sins, or even
recall them]; He will exult over you with
singing.*

o Never become complacent in your
relationship with the Holy Spirit.
Always seek to go deeper and higher in
learning and growing in Him. If you find
yourself becoming complacent or stagnant,
search out what may be blocking you from
shifting deeper. Blockages could be fear,
insecurity, not feeling in control, a curse or
stronghold, unforgiveness, and sin issues.
Control is a big hindrance to going deeper. In
order to truly grow in God and reach destiny,
we have to surrender in trusting and totally

being vulnerable in Him. Spend time commanding your spirit to go higher and deeper in your relationship with the Holy Spirit.

➤ Repent for any areas you have not relinquished control or have not submitted your will to God.

➤ Repent for fears of giving up control and release forgiveness to anyone that you have given control of your life, but they have misused or taken advantage of your trust.

➤ Build your trust in God by decreeing out scriptures in the areas of trust, faith and belief if necessary, as this will further cleanse any blockages, walls and lingering strongholds in this area. I usually cleanse by soaking in the blood of Jesus. I command the blood to cleanse all the effects of strongholds, while commanding any spirits behind it to go. I then spend time soaking in the healing glory of God.

➤ Study scriptures on going higher and deeper, and on healing. Meditate on them as you are commanding your spirit to go higher and deeper.

➤ Ask the Holy Spirit what is the next phase of intimacy with Him and to give you tools to work on to cultivate and accelerate into that next level of relationship

o If you do not speak in your prayer language, ask the Holy Spirit to give you

your prayer language. Spend time daily
building yourself up by speaking in
tongues.

o   Speaking in tongues is a gift. You do not
    have to work by tarrying for it. If you
    study tarrying, it is simply waiting on the
    Holy Spirit to empower you, and if you
    have been pursuing the Holy Spirit as your
    friend, then you are already spending time
    waiting and resting in His presence.

o   Speaking in tongues truly is a faith act of
    opening your mouth and speaking as the
    Holy Spirit leads. Through our prayer
    language, comes an increased power and
    guidance of the Holy Spirit to speak the
    voice of God, operate in giftings and live a
    life of holiness. Without the evidence of
    tongues one is basically living the actions of
    the intimacy and comfort of the Holy Spirit
    without the actual intimacy and love
    language of having the Holy Spirit
    indwelling in their lives. One thing we will
    learn from our relationship with the Holy
    Spirit is that intimacy is power. It is
    motivating, refreshing, reviving,
    strengthening, and accelerating (just think
    about how you feel when you are with
    someone you love). Though one may have
    the Holy Spirit, without the evidence of
    speaking in tongues, one is limited in their
    ability to express their feelings to God and
    God express Himself through them as the

Holy Spirit maketh intercession for us through groanings that we can't express or explain through our earthly comprehension or our earthly expressions.

Romans 8:26
Likewise the Spirit also helpeth our infirmities: for we know not what we should pray for as we ought: but the Spirit itself maketh intercession for us with groanings which cannot be uttered.

Also without speaking in tongues one is limited only to their native or learned language which is truly a soulish experience. But tongues liberate a person from the soulish to the spirit realm where they can be empowered to experience God and His mysteries on levels that the soul cannot go. This is not about the soul being carnal, but is just about when we operate in our soul, we tend to operate in our mind, will, and intellect so we operate in this realm we tend to limit things by what we know or what feels good or what feels comfortable. However, when we operate in God from Spirit to Spirit, we are more apt to be submissive to the unknowing. All our earthly boundaries are removed and we are inside a realm of unlimited potential, where His spirit is guiding and controlling our experience in God rather than we ourselves, being in control.

Speaking in tongues elevates a believer to a place in God such that the word says God will begin to reveal mysteries to us. These mysteries cannot be revealed or even understood by those who do not have the evidence of speaking in tongues.

> **1Corinthians 14:2**
> *For he that speaketh in an unknown tongue speaketh not unto men, but unto God: for no man understandeth him; howbeit in the spirit he speaketh mysteries.*

> **The Message Version**
> *If you praise him in the private language of tongues, God understands you but no one else does, for you are sharing intimacies just between you and him.*

Hindrances to not immediately speaking in tongues:
➤ Fear of the manifestation of tongues itself
➤ Fearing the mysteries of the process of speaking in tongues
➤ Fear of being vulnerable (losing control) and submitting to the presence of God and giving up their need to be in control or fear of being vulnerable before others
➤ Fear of how they will sound or what others will say
➤ Fear of the intimacy of tongues because one has to surrender and be intimate with God in order to yield themselves to the experience of the Holy Spirit. The 120 was

lingering…they were just waiting around for God. They deemed Him worth the wait. Many do not know how to be intimate, therefore, they fail to tap into a place of receiving.

➤ Tradition and religious beliefs

➤ Ignorance or lack of knowledge and understanding

➤ Not feeling worthy of God's gift

➤ Sin blockage or shame and guilt/condemnation still being present due to past or present sin in one's life.

➤ Demonic stronghold

➤ Fortune Telling, Satanism, Witchcraft, Horoscopes, Ouija Boards, Spiritism, or other non-Christian religions practices that need to be renounced. You see, the occult involvement in our lives was not innocent child's play. It breaks the First Commandment and gives Satan legal access to our lives. (Deuteronomy 18:10-12) If one is now going to seek supernatural guidance from God by His Holy Spirit, then they need to silence all other occult influences in Jesus' Name. (Acts 19:19) They may even need to destroy all objects in their home or life that have supernatural ties. God speaks through our hearts not through mediums or objects.

➤ Atmosphere may not be conducive to being able to receive (you however can create an atmosphere by praising and worshiping or declaring the scriptures)

➢ Or it is not time to receive yet. Like the 120, the Holy Spirit may want to build up anticipation, faith, and/or relationship before manifesting the evidence of tongues.

Ask the Holy Spirit to discern the reason and keep building a relationship with Him, while asking Him to give your prayer language. He will not leave you desiring.

> ### Luke 11:13
> *If you then, who are evil, know how to give good gifts to your children, how much more will the heavenly Father give the Holy Spirit to those who ask him!*
>
> ### Ephesians 5:18-21
> *And do not get drunk with wine, for that is debauchery, but be filled with the Spirit, addressing one another in psalms and hymns and spiritual songs, singing and making melody to the Lord with your heart, giving thanks always and for everything to God the Father in the name of our Lord Jesus Christ, submitting to one another out of reverence for Christ.*
>
> ### Psalms 84:11
> *For the LORD God is a sun and shield: the LORD will give grace and glory: no good*

*thing will he withhold from them that walk
uprightly*

2Corinthians 1:20
*For all the promises of God in him are yea,
and in him Amen, unto the glory of God by
us.*

**<u>This insert is one of my MENTEE'S responses after
studying this chapter:</u>** *The first thing that shook me in
this chapter was reading about how the experiences with
the Holy Spirit are making us feel good in our flesh and
emotions, but we leave out of services unchanged because
we lack a true Spirit to Spirit encounter. This alone takes
me back to my "Playa Playa Days," when I would be with
men to make myself feel good rather it be just the sex (NO
STRINGS NO INTIMACY), or because he was paying the
bills, or taking me shopping or something (cause he made it
worth my while). Reading it that sounds so whorish but
that was me, it was my truth. What I use to do reminds me
of the mentality with having emotional pleasures with the
Holy Spirit, but no true change or exchange (OUCH and
AMEN).*

*The article goes on to say "this is because we are just
encountering the presence of the Holy Spirit, but lack true
relationship with the Him." According to that comment
we do intimate things with the Holy Spirit like flirt a little,
talk to Him in a manipulative kind of way, but when it
comes to allowing Him to go deep into who we are (all of
you/me) you/we pull out (OUUUUCH).*

*Exploring the friendship part of the chapter; I use to hear
old people say "there's not a friend like "Jesus." I often
wondered what they meant. I will be honest and say that*

*the whole friendship thing even in my thirties is new to me.
I am a social person. I generally love to be around people,
but other times, I can feel alone or lonely in a crowded
room. I always ask the Lord, "how can a married woman
with people who adore her, feel this way." I am guessing it
is because I haven't allowed to the Holy Spirit to be a friend
to me (kind of hard to wrap my mind around...it may take a
moment or two).*

*In the natural, I do not call too many people my best friend.
Although I have a few that call me that, I tend to be very
leery of people, and it is because of my past experiences in
and out of the kingdom of God. I am not making an excuse,
just laying a little foundation and facts. I know that I do
desire healthy whole relationships with people, so I have to
get this together (WITH THE HELP OF THE LORD).
With Him there will be no need unmet, no void left
unfilled. I remember a few months ago I was discussing
that I felt like I had a blockage in the spirit realm and I
could not really explain it but I think that this is it. All of
the years of hurt, pain, and not allowing the Holy Spirit to
be the "B all" in my life, is probably my blockage to
relationships and really trusting people with my heart.*

Also this passage of scripture made me sad:

> *"And though we are the ones who are to know Him,
> the Holy Spirit is constantly spurned and ostracized
> because of His position in our lives. Every time we
> dreadfully or lustfully wish for someone else or
> something else without initially drawing into the
> Holy Spirit, we reject, grieve and ostracized the
> Holy Spirit. For it is as if the one gift Jesus left to
> comfort us and be with us forever, we reject over
> and over and over and over again."*

*My whole childhood was one abandonment after the other.
I suffered years of abuse and I always used to wonder why
the Lord never sent someone to save me, to deliver me. It
made me kind of bitter at God and the church. I felt like
how come all of these prophets in here can see everything,
but me sitting here wounded and bleeding. Back then I
could not even grasp God, let alone the Holy Spirit being
anything to me. It was not taught, yet I remember all of
those feelings I had are probably what the Holy Spirit felt
like when I felt that way.*

*I remember when I met my dad (one time) and he spent the
weekend with me. He told me he was going to the store and
somehow I knew he wasn't coming back. That moment
hurt, but after reading this chapter, I asked the Holy Spirit
where He was, and the Holy Spirit said He was the one
who told me that my dad was not coming back. I can
remember times where I was so depressed and wanted to
end it all. I even drank bleach and nothing worked. I
didn't have to go to the hospital or anything. I asked the
Holy Spirit where He was during this experience, and He
said that He was the reason I did not die or get sick. I can
remember a time where I was beaten so bad (tortured). I
asked the Holy Spirit where He was and He said He took
more hits than I did. The Holy Spirit has always been my
friend even when I did not know it. I learned so much from
this chapter and it healed and affirmed so much in my spirit
and kingdom walk. It is going to be an ongoing tool for me
to use to grow closer to the Holy Spirit.*

Questions for Spiritual Exploration:

1. What reasons did Jesus send the Holy Spirit to us?
2. What did you learn about the importance of being a friend to the Holy Spirit?
3. List five ways to cultivate your friendship with the Holy Spirit?
4. What did you learn about having a Spirit to Spirit relationship with God?
5. What did you learn about speaking in your prayer language?

References:

Dictionary.com
Strong's Concordance
The Holy Bible

Cover Design and Layout:

Book Picture Cover and layout design by Reenita
Keys

Connect with her via Facebook